SHROPSHIRE SAINT
The Wesley Historical Lecture, No. 26

JOHN FLETCHER
from the portrait by J. Jackson, R.A.

SHROPSHIRE SAINT

*A Study in the Ministry and Spirituality of
Fletcher of Madeley*

by
GEORGE LAWTON
*Formerly Assistant-Curate
of Madeley, Shropshire*

WIPF & STOCK · Eugene, Oregon

Wipf and Stock Publishers
199 W 8th Ave, Suite 3
Eugene, OR 97401

Shropshire Saint
A Study in the Ministry and Spirituality of Fletcher of Madeley
By Lawton, George
Copyright©1960 Methodist Publishing - Epworth Press
ISBN 13: 978-1-4982-0493-4
Publication date 8/22/2014
Previously published by Epworth Press, 1960

"Every effort has been made to trace the current copyright
owner of this publication but without success. If you have any
information or interest in the copyright, please contact the publishers."

Contents

	ACKNOWLEDGEMENT	vi
	INTRODUCTION	vii
	FLETCHER'S WORKS	xv
1.	FRAMEWORK OF LIFE	1
2.	PARISH PRIEST OF ECCLESIA ANGLICANA	13
3.	LITERARY VOCATION	34
4.	CHRISTIAN THINKER	66
5.	SPIRITUAL DIRECTOR	95
	CONCLUSION	131
	INDEX	133

Acknowledgement

THE AUTHOR desires to express his gratitude especially to two persons: to his wife, who has shared these studies from the outset and for reducing an enigmatic manuscript to a neat typescript, and to the Rev. Wesley F. Swift, who believed in this book when as yet there was none of it, and for helping with the proofs.

Introduction

JOHN FLETCHER has numerous biographers. Even so, it is likely that the best is yet to be. That he is a fascinating subject for biographical study, hardly needs saying. Those who are interested will find proof of it in any of the works in the short list following:

1. 1786. Wesley, John. *Short Account of the Life and Death of the Revd John Fletcher* (Wesley's *Works* (1829), Vol. XI).
2. 1806. Benson, Joseph. *Life of Fletcher* (Volume I of Fletcher's *Works*).
3. 1822. Cox, Robert. *Life of the Rev. John William Fletcher.*
4. 1882. Tyerman, Luke. *Wesley's Designated Successor.*
5. 1885. Macdonald, F. W. *Fletcher of Madeley.*
6. 1902. Marrat, J. *The Vicar of Madeley: A Biographical Study.*
7. 1905. Allen, Brigadier Margaret. *Life of Fletcher* (Salvation Army Publishing Department).
8. n.d. Fletcher, John. *Short Account of the Life and Death of Rev. John Fletcher* (Derby and London.)
9. Accounts in booklet form and as periodical articles are innumerable, as are those in serious works of historical scholarship. The following are typical:
    (a) 1843. Burns, J. *Brief Sketch of the Character of the Rev. John Fletcher of Madeley.* (Chapter 5 of his *Life of Mrs John Fletcher.*)
    (b) 1869. Ryle, J. C. (Bishop) *Fletcher of Madeley and his Ministry.* (In the *Family Treasury:* later included in Ryle's *Christian Leaders of the Last Century.*)

(c) 1872. Gregory, Dr Benjamin. *Papers on Fletcher.* (In *City Road Magazine.*)

(d) 1908. *Churches in our Patronage: VII.—Madeley, Salop.* (In the Church Pastoral Aid Society's Magazine—based on the Society's earlier booklet, *The Mecca of Methodism.*)

Wesley's account is a wonderfully objective, yet heartfelt tribute to Fletcher's abilities, charm, achievements, evangelical ministry and spotless purity of Christian piety.

Benson's life has the merits of incorporating many Fletcher letters, besides having Mrs Fletcher's special assistance. It is based on original materials. He knew Fletcher personally, as did Wesley, of course. Benson had the sort of mind that would appreciate Fletcher's theological and philosophical learning, and his literary gifts.

Cox, the perpetual curate of St Leonard's Church, Bridgnorth, Shropshire, wrote a vivid account of Fletcher. He preserves some of Fletcher's crisp sayings, and includes recollections of Fletcher's parishioners and clerical neighbours. He laments Fletcher's Methodist excesses, and gloomily alludes to his irregularities as a parish priest.

Tyerman's book has long been the standard biography. Its title singles out what the writer regarded as the highest testimony to Fletcher's qualities and worth, namely, that Wesley desired to commit to him the oversight of Methodism. Tyerman's work is thorough, well documented and scholarly, but somewhat heavy. It marks well chronological data, incident, personal contacts and publications (no mean achievement), but he allows no sidelights, and misses his hero's scintillating personality. From the critical angle Tyerman fails in not selecting the best of Fletcher's work, and in giving no indication when he telescopes passages in quotation. Sometimes paragraphs, and occasionally whole pages are omitted in this way.

Macdonald selects Fletcher's spirituality as his unique monument. He writes: 'For seraphic piety, for sanctity that had no perceptible flaw, Fletcher of Madeley stood alone.' But this writer surely had never looked deeply into Fletcher's mind, or he would never have said that Fletcher could not sustain comparison with Wesley regarding intellectual power. Certainly he could not marshal men as Wesley could, but his writings reveal him as Wesley's intellectual equal.

The little life by Marrat is good reading. Wesley's *Life of Fletcher* fired him in youth with an enthusiastic hero-worship, so that, as he confesses, Fletcher had for him ever after 'a starry beauty'.

The Brigadier's volume is most novel in arrangement. All the odd-numbered chapters deal with Fletcher, and all the even-numbered ones with Mary Bosanquet, in parallel periods up to their marriage. Churchmen, Anglican and Methodist, will be jarred by the remarks of Commissioner Railton in his Introduction. It is only what is 'red hot' in Fletcher that he recommends. He writes: 'It must not, however, . . . be imagined that Salvationists can conceive of a red-hot life mixed with the reading of prayers out of a book, or the teaching of any poor soul to turn to such heathenish folly.' O to have heard Fletcher's comment on that! He believed his Liturgy to be the finest in the world—and in any case, he exceedingly feared heat without light.

Of the shorter accounts mention is made here of two only, i.e. those by Burns and Ryle. Burns's is typical of many little narratives which quote at length the material of Wesley, Mrs Fletcher, and Joshua Gilpin, with hardly a note of query or dissent. The last chapter in Burns's volume comprises selections from Fletcher's Sermons and posthumous remains which, it is claimed, had not been published in the regular editions of the *Works*.

Bishop Ryle's paper of two chapters is a challenge to the almost reverential estimates which prevail, as though by conspiracy, in finding nothing to criticize. Concerning the circumstances of Fletcher's ordination the Bishop seems astonished. As to his parochial ministry, Ryle truly discerns that the machinery which Fletcher used was 'very simple and apostolic'. He rates Fletcher a man of burning zeal, to have reached the highest point of Christian excellence in his ability to suffer, and to sit still and wait as the prisoner of God's providence. But Ryle is unhappy about Fletcher the controversialist. On the one hand he fears Fletcher's reputation as a writer will not stand so high as it deserves, because of the controversial form. On the other hand, he thinks that the controversy itself was largely with shadows of Fletcher's own raising. 'The Calvinist antagonists hated Antinomianism and unholy living as much as Fletcher did', says the Bishop. Furthermore, Ryle suspects that Fletcher was not such an Arminian as he thought he was, and that he afterwards regretted some of the things which he uttered in the heat of the day. He is, the Bishop allows, a very able adversary—making the best that can be made of a bad cause.

These comments upon the little bibliography given above, illustrate the need for the chapters that follow. The interest shown in Fletcher by men of widely different schools of religious thought suggests a rare richness in his personality. Sectarianism wants Fletcher's zeal without the wisdom of the Church. Anglicanism is prone to honour the man as a shining instance of the piety summed up by Richard Baxter in his saying, 'As thou wilt, when thou wilt, where thou wilt', but is not usually prepared to study his (Fletcher's) writings. Methodism is naturally interested chiefly in Fletcher the Methodist but is often unfamiliar with the Establishment, and is liable to shelve the difficult tracts of Fletcher's thought. Tyerman, for instance, admits in his Preface: 'I have refrained from discussing the truths which Fletcher's pen defended, but I have said enough to indicate what the doctrines were which created Methodism, and which alone can perpetuate its spiritual life and power.'

There are four main roles in Fletcher's career, which need to be examined, and examined together; they are those of parish minister, author, theologian (or Christian philosopher), and director of souls. We do this in the following chapters, more in the hope that it will convince Anglicans and Methodists of the fruitfulness of the field, than in the belief that the need itself is here met.

The first chapter is the merest outline of the outward events of Fletcher's life with the object of showing how he came to be what he was. The inner side of his life is not disclosed, as in Wesley's case, through diary and journal. There are singular difficulties in coming to grips with Fletcher's own religious experience, particularly with what can only be called his mysticism. To call one man a mystic, and at the same time an exemplary parish priest after the apostolic model, a tenacious controversialist, a theologian, and an experienced guide of souls, is a tax upon our credulity. Yet there is no other explanation of some states of Fletcher's consciousness in so far as we can enter into them from the hints he gives, than to rank him amongst the mystics. What else would make sense of this, for instance?—'A lesson I learn daily is to see things and persons in their *invisible root* and in their *eternal principle;* where they are not subject to change, decay and death: but where they blossom and shine in the primeval excellence allotted them by their gracious Creator. By these means I learn to walk by faith, and not by sight; but like a child instead of walking straight and firm in this good, spiritual way, I am still apt to cling here or there; which makes me cry: "Lord, let me see all things more clearly, that I may never mistake a shadow for the substance, nor put any creature, no not for a moment, in the place of the Creator; who deserves to be loved, admired, and sought after with all the powers of our souls." [1]

On one of the rare occasions when Fletcher was reflecting on his inner experience he used the language of advanced mysticism thus: 'I was favoured, like Moses, with a supernatural discovery of the glory of God, in an ineffable converse with him; so that whether I was then in the body, or out of the body, I cannot tell.'[2] He seems to have had flashes of illumination as he meditated upon his literary work. He wrote to Charles Wesley concerning the *Essay on Truth:* 'I had some weeks ago one of those touches which realize, or rather spiritualize the letter.'[3]

It may be doubted whether sufficient material exists for a satisfactory study of Fletcher's mysticism. But it seems probable that mystical experience (beyond the exercise of critical reason during the experience) might account for some difficulties in Fletcher's story. The most remarkable of these is the hardly credible utterance at the Conference-period of 1781: 'I am freed from sin.'[4] If this were the utterance of reason or reflection it is absolutely out of keeping with Fletcher's habitual humility, and his constant emphasis upon that grace. If, however, the experience in which it is reputed to have occurred was one of those heavenly 'touches' (and we have Mrs Fletcher's word for it that he had these mystical experiences in Church—presumably in public) then this dangerous utterance means that he enjoyed unimpeded communion with God. It is not, on this showing, to be taken as a theological dictum. Especially is this so in view of the fact that only eight weeks before, Fletcher had written: 'The work of sanctification is hindered ... by holding out the being *delivered from sin* as the mark to be aimed at

---

[1] *Works*, I.347.   [2] Ibid. p. 215.   [3] Ibid. p. 181.
[4] See Sangster, *Path to Perfection*, pp. 32 and 162ff.

instead of the being *rooted in Christ* and being *filled with the fullness* of God.'[5]

Charles Wesley, apparently, with characteristic realism, never lost sight of the human Fletcher in his veneration of the saint. A letter preserved in the MS. *Life of Joseph Benson*[6] indicates that even towards the end of Fletcher's life, Charles was not too sure of his friend's 'advisableness'. Charles writes to Mrs Fletcher: 'He is (I know and he knows) a mule by nature; but is become by grace, and by the wisdom from above, easy to be entreated.' Charles says that Mrs Fletcher alone can save her husband from working himself to premature death.

A man so mystical, yet so energetic is surely a challenge to any biographer, and indeed to anyone writing about him. Fletcher cannot be precisely classified and labelled. He is above sectarian consistency. His name generally evokes the picture of a saintly clergyman struggling with a rowdy parish in troublous times. This he was; but he was much more. It would be nearer the mark to think of him as a genius in the great company of the saints.

---

[5] *Works*, I.311.   [6] Given in *Wesley Historical Society Proceedings*, XI.18.

Fletcher's Works

(a) Chief Writings, as they appeared

Undated, but early; published posthumously. *The Spiritual Manifestation of the Son of God.*[1]

1771. *First Check to Antinomianism.*
,, *Second Check to Antinomianism.*

1772. *Third Check to Antinomianism.*
,, *Fourth Check to Antinomianism.*
,, *Appeal to Matter of Fact.*

1773. *A Dreadful Phenomenon.* (Sermon on 'earthquake' which changed the course of the River Severn.)

1774. *Fictitious and Genuine Creed.*
,, *Fifth Check to Antinomianism.*
,, *Equal Check to Pharisaism and Antinomianism: Part I* (containing *Essay on Truth*).

1775. *Equal Check to Pharisaism and Antinomianism: Part II* (containing *Scripture Scales, Part I,* and *The Reconciliation*).
,, *Equal Check to Pharisaism and Antinomianism: Part III* (containing *Scripture Scales, Part II*).
,, *Last Check to Antinomianism* (containing *A Polemical Essay*).

1776. *Vindication of Wesley's Calm Address.*
,, *Answer to Toplady's Vindication of the Decrees.*
,, *American Patriotism.*

[1] For the influence of this work upon Hugh Bourne, founder of Primitive Methodism, see *Wesley Historical Society Proceedings*, XXVIII. 131-7.

1777. *Reply to Principal Arguments. . . . Remarks on Toplady's Scheme of Christian and Philosophical Necessity.*

1778(*c.*) *Discourse on the New Birth.*

1776–81. Poem in French entitled *La Louange*—Enlarged and published in England 1785. English Translation by Miles Martindale entitled *Nature and Grace*.

„ „ *Portrait of St Paul* (in French)—English Translation by Joshua Gilpin (1790).

1784. *Rational Vindication of the Catholic Faith* (possibly unfinished. Edited by Joseph Benson).

(*b*) *Some Editions of the Collected Works*

Numerous editions since 1800: e.g.

1803. London. 8 Vols. 12mo.

1806. London. 8 Vols. 8vo. Edited by Joseph Benson. (Volume I is Benson's *Life of Fletcher*, also issued separately. Volume IX, Supplementary —1808.) The Index in Vol. VIII was prepared by Samuel Taylor. Benson desired one for Vol. IX, but for some reason unknown it never appeared.[2]

1825. London. 7 Vols. 24 mo.

1826. London. 7 Vols. 18mo.

1836. London. 7 Vols. 12mo.

1851. New York. 4 Vols. Medium 8vo.

[2] *Wesley Historical Society Proceedings*, XXX.60.

(c) *Selections of Works*

1829. 2 Vols. by A. Scot (with a Life).

1843. London. 2 Vols. 8vo. Edited by J. Burns, Minister of Marylebone.

N.B.—All references to Fletcher's *Works* here are to Benson's 1806–8 Edition.

CHAPTER ONE

Framework of Life

1. 'THE LITTLE MARKET TOWN OF MADELEY'

TWO HUNDRED years ago, on Friday 17th October 1760 to be precise, a foreigner who had Englished his name into John William Fletcher, who already had a local reputation for upsetting congregations and to whom the stigma of being a Methodist was attached, was inducted to the temporalities of Madeley in the north-east quarter of Shropshire. He had been instituted to the cure of souls of that parish at the Bishop's Palace at Hereford a few days before. Thus, without episcopal visitation and probably without any formal ceremony, began one of the most remarkable parochial ministries in the history of the Church of England.

It was this clergyman who put the name Madeley on the ecclesiastical map. Outlying parts of this parish achieved fame during his incumbency and just afterwards, apart altogether from Fletcher, but not Madeley itself. The renowned Coalport China was produced in the mushroom colony of kilns and huts of that name which clustered on the Severn bank hundreds of feet below the Church. They could imitate Sèvres ware so well that their ceramic experts have unwittingly bought back their own products for the Works' Sèvres display cabinet. At other points of the parish, notably at Coalbrookdale, the 'Iron Men' were leading the world in methods of processing iron, and were working wonders in casting it. Many cottages had upon their walls at least one cast-iron ornamental piece—a country scene or a tracery-pattern plate. The larger houses had a casting of da Vinci's

'Last Supper', all with lines as clear as if they had been etched. The parish associated iron with death as well as with life. Many of the tombstones in the churchyard were, inscription and all, of cast iron. A few coffins even were of cast iron. Did not iron-mad Wilkinson carry his around with him to different parts of England? What delicious ironies would have dropped from Fletcher's pen if he could have known the sequel: Wilkinson's executors refused the burden of his cherished casket.

Cast iron had its world-première show in Madeley parish. The first cast-iron bridge sprang across the Severn from Fletcher's boundary, and not far away was launched the first iron barge. It has been claimed that the first cast-iron rail-road ran across the coal seams in the parish, and there was an oak railroad worn out long before that. A barge-lifting incline built in connection with early canal systems gave the parish a place in the annals of marine engineering. Other features were almost as remarkable—for instance the blowing apparatus which looked like the pleasure-wheel of a modern fair-ground, used in the production of pig iron. Economic and philanthropical, as well as industrial experiments were conducted in Madeley parish by the Quaker Iron-Masters.

Coal getting had been carried on here since the year 1322. Whole neighbourhoods were riddled burrow-fashion with shallow tunnels which broke the surface in innumerable scars. In other places the pits were deep for those days. A line drawn from the Church towards the Wrekin passed through a weary conglomeration of forges, furnaces and pits. In these last-named, the 'cage' was raised and lowered by a cable worked in a 'whimsey' by a horse going round and round.

The conjunction of water, coal, ironstone and limestone rendered Madeley a land of opportunity for the Industrialists. The Severn was navigable up to Shrewsbury in Fletcher's day. The work that followed in their

SAINT 3

wake turned the parish into an unholy Midland Mecca for bargemen, furnacemen, miners, quarrymen, watermen and wagoners.

In spite of the industrial blots on the parish landscape, Madeley was largely agricultural. It was, as Fletcher said, 'a little market town'. It was not without charm. The River Severn forming its Western boundary flows part of the way through a deep wooded valley. The huge ribs of the iron bridge make a surprisingly neat frame for an attractive scene looking either way. Coracles may be seen in its shadow to this very day. High above the bridge, standing in the garden of a modern vicarage which serves one of the parishes carved out of Fletcher's parish, there is a vista looking up-river which suggests the smaller Swiss valleys. Coalbrookdale even today is not destitute of all its wooded charm. From the high cliffs above the Severn the terrain falls away eastwards and southwards into tracts of farm land.

Madeley was not all huts, hovels, slag-heaps and gin shops. It retained much of the atmosphere of the English manor, especially around the Church, where fine medieval and Elizabethan buildings still exist.[1]

II. FLETCHER OF MADELEY

Who was this man who turned Madeley into 'the Mecca of Methodism', as it has been called? When he became Vicar at the age of thirty-one he had been in England only eight years. For the first eighteen months of this period he took duty at a boarding-school in Hertfordshire, but his chief concern was to become proficient in the English language. The other six-and-a-half years he had spent as tutor to the wealthy Shropshire family of Hill of Tern

[1] For medieval Madeley see Eyton, *Antiquities of Shropshire*. For Industrial Madeley see *Salopian Monthly Illustrated Journal* 1875-6 (a Work issued from Madeley); Smiles, *Lives of the Engineers;* Ashton and Sykes, *The Coal Industry in the Eighteenth Century;* Court, *The Rise of the Midland Iron Industries; Transactions of the Newcomen Society*, Vols. IV and V.

Hall (modern Attingham House), a fine mansion on the fields of Haughmond Abbey. It is still to be seen, set back from the Severn in parkland four miles south-east of Shrewsbury. Today it is a College of Further Education.

As tutor, Fletcher moved about with the family. During most of the Parliamentary sessions he was in London. In 1754, on one of the journeys to the capital, the tutor was looking round St Albans when he came across an old woman whose conversation on the love of God so gripped him that he missed the coach. When he rejoined the family it was to be made the butt of a jocular reference to Methodism. Methodist prayerfulness proved to be, for Fletcher, an important clue to be followed in unravelling the mystery of his own soul. He joined the St Albans Methodists whenever he could. He also met the Wesleys in London. From childhood he had been of a serious and deeply religious turn of mind. During his late teens, at the University of Geneva, his religion was more a philosophy than a culture of the heart. Before the simple Methodist woman unwittingly showed him his empty heart, he loved to think and meditate as he strolled in the pastures on the banks of the Severn. But the faith that brought release and peace eluded him. He was in thrall to rational endeavours to translate à Kempis into his own life and circumstances. Then, early in 1755, in his twenty-sixth year, he was set free from mental agony. Passing through the terrors of the Lord, mostly in dreams, he experienced a conversion. Here we simply record it as an important point in the framework of his life, and make one comment. It was, once again, the *love* of God which struck him. It evoked his 'saving faith'. When it had sunk into his consciousness he slid quietly into peace as a child drops into the warmth and safety of its evening rest.

For two years after his conversion Fletcher spent a lot of time with the London Methodists. Then his employer, influential and with Church patronage in his own gift, anticipating Fletcher's release as his pupils grew up, offered to help him into the Ministry of the Church of England. It was nearly two years however, before Fletcher could with mental honesty present himself for Ordination. To be ordained deacon and priest in the space of eight days by different diocesan bishops suggests that Fletcher was no ordinary candidate. It seems that he was not ordained to a specific assistant-curacy. On the day that he was ordained to the priesthood he turned up at Snowsfields Chapel from the mountains of Switzerland, so it seemed to Wesley, and helped in a lengthy celebration of Holy Communion.

From March 1757 to October 1760 Fletcher made a name for himself as a preacher amongst the Methodists. In impassioned English, if with an intriguing foreign touch and using quaint constructions, he moved his audiences to tears or else electrified them with fears. He preached in French also—this was his native tongue—with equal success. As a humble aristocrat, as a young man of great charm and courtesy, as a man of culture possessed of a nimble mind, he was considered a capture by London Methodism. And indeed so he was, but he was even more so for his spirituality. Ever after his conversion this man lived conspicuously but unselfconsciously in the suburbs of heaven; it was acknowledged on all hands that there was something angelic about him.

Much of Heaven, as well as many of his gifts and graces, lay about him in his childhood and youth. He had a favoured start. He was born on 12th September 1729 at Nyon in Switzerland into a military family of distinction. Late in life, and only then under pressure, he disclosed that his family possessed rank similar to that of an English earldom. He grew up on his father's estate, which contained expansive lake, woodland and hill scenery. He drew back his curtains each morning to behold 'one of the finest prospects in the world'. He breathed the bracing air of a Protestantism better than its creed, i.e. of a Calvinism which, whilst fearing God, was not afraid of His gifts or even of creating wealth. In this domestic atmosphere of order, culture and security, the logical issues of 'the horrible decree' of Predestination rarely appeared. Young Jean Gillaume de la Flechère felt something of the love of God in his childhood. It was an understood thing in his home that the Ministry of the Church was to be his destiny. For this he prepared at Geneva by an arduous seven-years course. Academically, he carried all before him. Then came a hitch. Calvin's doctrine of Election, he now saw, hid a cloven hoof. He could not proceed to ordination because he could not without mental reservation subscribe to the Articles of his Church.

Like many another saint, military life had attractions for him. Two determined attempts to enlist, against the will of his parents, were frustrated, one in Spain by a scalded foot, and the other in Holland by the death of his sponsor. And so he turned to England. He arrived in 1752, just one more alien; he soon became as thoroughgoing a supporter of the English Constitution as John Wesley himself.

III. WHAT MANNER OF MAN?

This outline of Fletcher's career so far, that is up to his residence in Madeley in 1760, leaves one little gap to be filled. For the three years following his ordination as priest he remained a free-lance clergyman. He gives a hint that he was still testing his conversion. The period affords such instances of his spirit, notably of his humility, that it will serve to introduce the subject of his personality. We thus notice a few facts concerning his physical frame, his mental attainments and his Christian experience.

Fletcher had captivated the London Methodists, Wesley included, but the unleavened congregations around Shrewsbury proved to be very different. Neither his charm nor his originality, his dynamism nor his service for the logic of truth could break down their resistance. He was rarely asked back to the parish churches a second time. If in this period Madeley was the exception, it was probably because that rough parish was considered no catch. Had the parish officers had any idea that he would shortly displace their easy-going parson, they would have cold-shouldered him from the outset. On the other hand, the fact that only at Madeley did he do spells of duty may account for his readiness to settle there. For Madeley had cast some sort of spell over Fletcher, but there seemed not the remotest chance that he would go there. He was offered a quiet, well-paid living by the father of his pupils, but he turned it down. The patron was astounded and bewildered at Fletcher's preference for Madeley, but in the end he offered his little plum to the Vicar of Madeley, who changed his anti-Methodist tune and gladly moved out in order to let the quixotic Swiss Methodist move in.

Fletcher had borne clerical animosity and lay mistrust with quiet dignity, waiting until God's way opened. When he was not teaching or preaching he would sit beside the farm labourers, and even beside the children in the Catechism class, humbly rejoicing in the love of Christ and striving to know more of it.

Madeley's new Vicar was a slight man of medium height. Of him it could be said that he had a lady's hand, a lion's heart and the eye of an eagle. So great was his reputation for holiness that his very body seemed ethereal. Yet he was no weakling. He often swam a five-mile stretch in his youth, and well on in his life, after he had lain at death's door several times, he swam daily whilst attending a Conference in Yorkshire. As Vicar of Madeley he rode in all weathers. He tramped his parish, he fasted, he gave away his food, he bolted it to save time for prayer, or he forgot to eat altogether. He buffeted his body, not so much to keep it under as because his soul was so much on top. He 'dropped his clay' long before he died, so translucent was his spirit.

We have referred to his education. What was his mental capacity? Perhaps the best evidence that we have lies in his voluminous writings. He was at home in the biblical writings—Hebrew and Greek. He was at home among the classics also. French was his mother-tongue and he learned German in his late teens. What he could do with English we shall see later on in this study. He had studied patristic and dogmatic theology. Like Wesley he was interested in 'natural philosophy'. Like Wesley also he was a logician. That eagle eye (it struck everybody) matched a remarkable mental clarity. He could pounce upon a fallacy as surely as a surgeon detects a foreign body. We shall trace the workings of his mind in the Chapter headed 'Christian Thinker'.

Fletcher was conscious that in some respects he stood in contrast to English ways. He frequently spoke of his 'Suisse plainness and honesty',[2] 'Helvetic bluntness',[3] 'Alpine roughness',[4] and so on. This cannot refer to discourtesy. He spoke and acted with the unselfconscious sincerity of good breeding. This bluntness was a mental rather than a cultural habit. Fletcher had been cradled, as he put it, in 'Suisse Reason'.[5] This might have reference to that Continental realism which is often contrasted with the sentimentality of much English life. Sometimes, however, Fletcher means moral honesty when he speaks of these Swiss characteristics. Unquestionably he was an utter stranger to that polite refinement of thought which Wesley consistently denounced as shuffling, twisting, turning, show and veneer. The lives of both men abound with instances of rebuke. One of the stories preserved of

[2] E.g. *Works*, III.326. [3] E.g. ibid. IV.94.
[4] E.g. ibid. V.209. [5] Ibid. III.65.

Fletcher's childhood tells how he exposed the inconsistent conduct of even his beloved mother in a way that admitted no evasion. All through his life he saw things, particularly human conduct, defined sharply and with no gradations, and out of this certainty he fearlessly denounced erroneous thought and evil conduct wherever and in whomsoever he found them.

So little is known about Fletcher's childhood that the raw material of his adult fame and achievements can only be guessed at, and one hesitates to do that. It is unlikely that his Calvinist, Alpine upbringing would dispose him to welcome the 'Merrie England' atmosphere of Madeley. The seeds of Fletcher's evangelicalism lie there perhaps. Again, Fletcher wrote things about children which many would regard as sickeningly misanthropic.[6] One might hazard the guess that he had everything in his childhood except his share of natural affection. Perhaps even in childhood he fled from it; certainly in manhood for thirty years he stifled it. Natural ties had but little hold upon him. He admitted that his relatives in Switzerland often urged him to return, but he replied that he must obey God rather than men. And so he left his 'sentry box', as he called his post at Madeley, very rarely.

IV. VICAR FOR TWENTY-FIVE YEARS

Self-abandonment to, and self-restriction in the Cause of God characterized the rest of his life, his whole incumbency of a quarter of a century in Shropshire. Gifted, charming, saintly, courageous—John Wesley wanted him for a nation-wide campaign. But Fletcher said 'The snail does best in his shell'. It was a pretty big shell really, though minute beside Wesley's world parish.

It is probable that if Wesley had succeeded in getting him mounted oftener, Fletcher might have lived longer. Wesley had absolute faith in a medicine which once was

---

[6] E.g. ibid. II.29-30.

proverbial, and believed that the best thing for the inside of a man was the outside of a horse. The best that Wesley could do was to persuade Fletcher to have a reminder inscribed upon a pane of glass in the study window thus:

> The wise for health on exercise depend,
> God never made his works for man to mend.

Fletcher undertook only one or two long evangelistic tours, but he was received as an apostle wherever Methodists gathered to meet him.

His parish work (we use the expression loosely here to mean his ministry in and around Madeley) was broken to any extent in three respects only. First, by repeated journeys into Wales from 1768 to 1771, during the period of his presidency of the theological college sponsored by Lady Huntingdon; secondly, by journeys relating to the Methodism of Wesley's Connexion; and thirdly, by an absence of four and a half years on the Continent, chiefly in Switzerland, fighting consumption.

It is not difficult to understand Wesley's chagrin at Fletcher's burying himself in a country parish. Nor is it difficult, the more we know of Fletcher, to understand his point of view. He was not really like Wesley deep down. Fletcher was a man without ambition and without drive as the world reckons these things. He was the humblest of the servants of God. His admiration for John Wesley was unbounded, but he never thought of imitating him. Although not a lover of ease, he often spoke of his 'beloved obscurity', sometimes in quaint expressions. Besides scriptural phrases such as 'worm of earth' and 'wishing oneself accursed' for the sake of God's glory, he would liken his own efforts to 'pipes' as contrasted with the 'trumpets' of Whitefield, and his prayers to 'dancing motes' as against the 'mountain of Christ's work'. He would gladly have been boot-black or postilion to men far inferior in rank and in spirituality; for instance, he compared himself unfavourably with Rowland Hill in the words—'What is an old Saul to a young David'. And again, he alluded to himself as 'a grindstone from the neighbourhood of the Alps' though his writings reveal a mind with a razor edge.

Here we discover this man's secret. Physical restriction did not exist for him because spiritually and mentally his life was so expansive. Here Wesley did draw Fletcher out. The mild Vicar broke through shell, sentry-box, beloved obscurity and all, to fight in the Calvinian Controversy in defence of Wesley and evangelical truth. His parochial ministry permitted long spells of study and the writing of numerous books and pamphlets. It is generally agreed that this was Fletcher's distinctive activity, and our studies here are mainly of the man as he reveals himself in his literary work.

His literary break-through itself is not without severe limitations. To critics like Sir Leslie Stephen it is but a ripple in a backwater. We shall make our own assessment later on, but a general reference to Fletcher's limitations may be made at this point. He admitted that he had never read Shakespeare. Later on in his life he said that he read little except the Bible. Except during his theological training it is probable that he was never an omnivorous reader. He spent more time praying than reading; he never needed the advice which Wesley thought good to give to Fletcher's biographer Benson—'throw away that thirst for books'. But his limitations in this respect only make his literary achievements the more remarkable.

There was something of the stoic in Fletcher—indeed he often alluded to himself as a 'Christian Stoic'. His twenty-one years bachelorhood at Madeley reflected this. And then, when he was fifty-one years old and in poor health, he capitulated to a love which had slumbered for twenty-four years. He could have swept Mary Bosanquet off her feet in his early manhood, when he had so much to give.

She shook his composure for months. It says something for them both that she did not refuse him in the evening of his life. They had just under four years of seraphic happiness together. He was only fifty-five when he died on 14th August 1785.

Over two thousand people—a number that represents two-thirds of the entire population of Fletcher's parish—stood around his grave. Many people wept unashamedly. The poor emaciated body was buried most fittingly between his vicarage and his church, the foci of his ministry. His tombstone is of cast-iron, with a lengthy inscription in relief. The Methodists and the Anglicans of Madeley take it in turns to care for the tomb.

Had Fletcher been a Roman Catholic, there would ere this have been a clamour for his canonization. His tomb would have become a shrine, and place of pilgrimage. Free Churchmen, and Anglicans to some extent, are prone to forget their saints. John Fletcher was a saint if ever there was one. The tributes paid at his death, and in almost all literary notices since, were in the superlative.

For about a century some work by Fletcher found a place beside those of à Kempis, Law and Wesley in Methodist homes. The twentieth century hardly knows his name. These studies commemorating the bicentenary of his Institution to the Cure of Souls in Madeley, draw out aspects of his life and work which are fundamental to a knowledge of the man, but which, the present writer believes, have not been thoroughly studied hitherto.

CHAPTER TWO

Parish Priest of Ecclesia Anglicana

1. INGLORIOUS INHERITANCE

THERE HAD been a vicar at Madeley since Norman times. Much of its church history was unenviable. As far back as 1243 the Prior of Madeley Manor (the parish was associated with Wenlock Abbey for over three hundred years) was served with a royal writ for trafficking in pardons to finance hunting. Few of the incumbents stayed long. Three served just over a year between them in 1299-1300. In the year 1322 there were three changes. There was a chapelry or chantry dedicated to the Virgin Mary erected in the Church in the reign of Richard II. Ostensibly it was maintained by lands or rents, but the vicar, who was himself ground by the Prior, in his turn pressed the Chaplain. The chapelry was dissolved by the Commissioners of Henry VIII. It frequently happened that the parish had only the impoverished ministrations of the chantry priest. Its position as a pawn of the Abbey Chapter was ironically indicated in its other designation, i.e. Prior's Madeley. For with every change of incumbency the prior exacted fees and fealty.

We have already seen that the parish was no plum in the eighteenth century. For centuries, prior to the Reformation and since, it had been a poor living. In 1369 the Rectorial tithes were valued at £5 per annum. In 1534 these had dropped to under £2. But it is recorded that the vicar's income had increased from £3 6s. 8d. to £5 5s. in that period. When the vicar and churchwardens visited every family to make a collection for the relief of Londoners after the Great Fire of 1666, they could gather no more than £1 2s. 10d. The value of the living when Fletcher became vicar was about £75 a year. But this was largely tithe in kind, and the account books indicate that frequently the 'tithe pig' or the 'tithe lamb' was owing.

Consequent upon the Industrial Revolution came a rapid influx of population. Archdeacon Plymley's *Survey of Shropshire* indicates that the increase was a thousand each decade during the period of Fletcher's ministry, so that at the time of his death the return was just over three thousand. This would increase the income in the matter of 'surplice fees'.

II. PARSONAGE HOUSE AND CHURCH

What was Fletcher's inheritance when he began his ministry in Madeley? His house had been built about 1670, and stands today practically unchanged in its external appearance and in its room-plan. Its accommodation was simplicity itself—four smallish rooms on each of three floors, two on each side of an oblong hall on the ground floor, and two on each side of identical landings above. This plain brick house must have been a striking contrast to the noble home of his boyhood. Quite often, indeed, he referred to it as 'My hermitage'. Opening off his bedroom on the church side of the house was a tiny dressing-room. This was his prayer chamber. Up to 1951, at least, the breath-soiled patch on the wall opposite to his *prie-dieu* remained just as it was when he died.

Fletcher's Parish Church was razed to the ground early in the nineteenth century and an octagon built on the site. Both the poverty and the godlessness of the parishioners were reflected in the condition of the church when he took over. By all accounts it had been a fine structure, Norman in style with a chancel about the same length as the nave. The size of the chancel probably reflected monastic influence.

SAINT 15

Above the central space where the transepts joined the nave was a tower containing six bells. Several of these were already two hundred years old at Fletcher's institution, and the peal was celebrated proverbially along with Weobley ale and Lemster [Leominster] ore, as being the best in the Diocese of Hereford. But the tower was in serious disrepair and it was taken down three years after Fletcher's death.

The major factor in the deterioration of the whole building would be the decay of the manor. The wonderful Madeley Court, to which the last Abbot of Wenlock retired, was split up, and in one portion lived the Darbys, who refused to pay the church rate, let alone continue the main burden of maintaining and adorning the church which the Brooke family had previously shouldered. Tombs of this latter family were in the church—some of the effigies, in Elizabethan costume, may be seen today weathering badly on the *outside* of the octagon walls.

Whatever treasures Fletcher's church contained have disappeared with scarcely a trace. Although Fletcher was not responsible for this, since the church was intact when he died, his ministry contributed to its dissolution. In this parish throughout his ministry and during the lifetime of his widow who survived him by thirty years, Methodism was centred upon the parish church. In most parishes the Church of England held on its way with the Methodists either hanging on to the mother like bewildered children, or else snapping at her heels in uncertain independence. But here, the 'Methodist Parson' as he was called, did not hesitate to speak of the Church of England as 'Our Holy Mother', or to withstand those who regarded her as a 'wicked stepmother'.[1] In this parish, therefore, Methodism was Church, and Church was Methodism, yet here Methodism was the preponderating influence. In no other parish in Britain did it transform the very

[1] Cf. *Works*, III.463, VI.265.

structure of the church building. It was Fletcher who paved the way for a 'preacher's church'. He needed seating accommodation for well over a thousand people. The best that could be done in the old Norman Church was to put the pulpit near a window and take the window out so that those outside could hear, if not see. Determined efforts to rebuild the church, if this was necessary structurally, were deemed unreasonable in view of the tremendous changes in the people's church-going habits. Here we have an indirect and easily-missed testimony to the amazing ministry of this man. Neither Church dignitaries diocesan or local, nor Church courts on these levels, felt themselves able to withstand the flood which broke with centuries-old tradition. Typical of much else was the Bishop of Hereford's prudent silence in reply to Fletcher's appeal about the cottage-meetings in his parish.

It is remarkable that so much of the old order has perished without trace. Of the last Abbot of Wenlock's tomb, of glass, stalls, screens, hangings, lectern and font, the octagon knows nothing. Only a small pulpit, a Jacobean communion table, the bells and a few memorial tablets, besides the effigies already mentioned, remain as links between the old edifice and the new.

III. CURE OF SOULS

We turn now to look at the parish of Madeley, not topographically, but as the sphere in which Fletcher was to exercise his cure of souls. The church was nowhere near the centre of the parish. This was because westward of the manor house, church, and village, large forests had been only slowly cleared. The clearance was speeded up in hamlets as much as four miles away from the church, by wood-fuel consumption in the early furnaces and forges. From these hamlets it was a long steep climb to what was called 'the Church Town'.

There would seem to have been no mission rooms or the like—this was one of Fletcher's provisions, culminating in a large chapel at Madeley Wood for which he found practically all the money, using income from properties in Switzerland.

Not far from the church was a Baptist Meeting and a Roman Catholic Chapel. A flourishing Quaker Meeting existed at Coalbrookdale. The first-mentioned seems to have been a small cause, and there is no evidence either that Fletcher was in conflict with it, or that it made any significant contribution to parish life. With regard to the other two things were very different.

To his dying day Fletcher remained a militant Protestant. The logical and theological grounds for this antagonism will be discussed in connection with our study of his thought. Just now we are concerned only with the fact and its expression. The Pope of Rome and all his enormities, indubitably the 'Scarlet Woman', was as a red rag to a bull to Fletcher whatever the circumstances and whatever the state of his health. Once, in Rome, it took the whole force of his friends to prevent what would have been a very ugly scene. Whilst seeking health in Switzerland and really ill at the time, he flogged himself into France to preach to the 'poor papists'.

At the very outset of his ministry in Madeley he joined issue with the Roman priest, although not exclusively with him on this occasion, ranking his system as 'Pharisaism' along with Nonconformist and Anglican formalism. He exposed Roman error in sermons in Church. Using a manuscript at this time, he probably was not so unguarded in church as on less formal occasions. His writings make quite clear what his 'Helvetic bluntness' was capable of when he was championing evangelical truth. In the calmness of the study he was roused to write such things as these: 'The impious absurdities of the Church of

Rome'; 'Saved—if he cordially kiss a crucifix and say *Ave Maria* at the stake'; 'The hocus-pocus of a Popish priest'; 'An idol of paste made by the baker and the priest'; 'Make, adore and swallow the wafer—god'; 'To pay divine honours to a bit of typical bread which their fancy had turned into the identical body of our Lord'; 'Poisoning the gospel truths with as many errors as the Church of Rome imposes upon her votaries'; 'The dirty channel of the Roman Church'. Some years later he admitted that it was unjust to condemn Roman Catholics in the lump. One of the kindest things he ever said about Rome was to admit that she may have three talents, but the compliment was immediately nullified as far as Roman Catholics were concerned by his conceit that Protestantism had four talents. He once spoke kindly of Catholic pilgrimages, urging a devout lady to pay a visit to Madeley in that spirit. For Fletcher, the thought of peaceful co-existence with Rome, in Madeley or anywhere else, was impossible. What he did not realize was that in England, especially in remote parts, the old Catholics lived quietly in the parishes, on the other side of the fence, but none the less members of communities which compromised for the sake of peace.

It was obviously the sheer vitality of Fletcher's impact upon his parish that blew up the sparks of Quaker concern for truth. There had been Quaker preaching in his parish long before his time. But not so long before his institution, Abiah Darby, daughter of one of the 'Iron Men', had been exercising an effective ministry all around the Wrekin. She was a woman of Susanna Wesley's calibre. Besides itinerating, she brought up children, studied the New Testament in Greek, wrote tracts and studied astronomy. She loathed the 'copyhold parsons', refused tithes, served the poor, and had a special concern for the education of children. Moreover, she had the knack of going for important people. We learn from her

Diary that she had a long discussion with Fletcher about Quaker principles only three months after he arrived. He borrowed Quaker books from her, and was still looking into the subject two years later. At this time Abiah sent up hopefully a book written by Richard Claridge, a priest who had been won to Quakerism from the Establishment, and with it a note: 'As thou hast always treated me with candour I have presumed to use freedom with thee. . . . I make free to say that I believe thou hast been of service in the Lord's hand to reform the people here away.'

Abiah, when moved thereto by the Spirit, would gatecrash into Fletcher's class-meetings and even into clerical synods. Accompanying Fletcher uninvited to a class-meeting at the house of George Cranage (who is remembered for inventing a new kind of reverberatory furnace), she felt she had to take up her cross, and, in her own words—'I had full time of it to declare against dead formality in religion. I had the mood [? word] to declare with power. I had close work of it for above three hours.' The *Diary* records that Fletcher made some objection, but 'behaved civil'. His patience is enshrined in her concluding sentence: 'We parted very friendly.'

Fletcher had been vicar for five years when Abiah got him to agree to discuss her latest booklet on the principles of religion at one of his meetings. She was invited, but did not go. At this meeting, unbeknown to Abiah, was one of her relatives, who reported that 'the parson read here a line, and there one, and made strange work of it'. The relative, one Daniel Rose, had to defend Abiah concerning what had been said at a previous meeting. Abiah writes into her *Diary* with relish, that Fletcher and his friends 'returned sharply "how could he [Rose] tell, not being present?", but he told them he was in the next room, which surprised them much'. Numerous lengthy arguments with Fletcher are recorded in Abiah's *Diary*, but less arduous visits to the vicarage are also noted, including one when Lady Huntingdon showed her great kindness.

IV. METHODIST AND ANGLICAN

With surprising industry and zeal Fletcher set about fulfilling his cure, maintaining its non-sectarian nature according to the Establishment. But early in his ministry he made an unfortunate appeal to law in defence of religious freedom in the matter of house-preaching, which taught him to appreciate the differences between the Church according to Constitution and actual Church life in the parishes. All the same, his admiration for the 'Elizabethan Settlement' and all it stood for, was unabated to the end of his life. The England of the Reformers is spoken of as if it were the Golden Age: sometimes he seems to regard it as fact, and at other times as a Reformer's dream. The Reforming English Fathers, and especially Cranmer, appear to him in patriarchal glory.[2] Thus he speaks of 'Our blessed Reformers',[3] 'Our own excellent Church',[4] 'Our excellent constitution'.[5] What he calls 'the suffrage of the Church of England'[6] is for him an authority next only to Scripture, and hardly less than that, since this suffrage had agreement with Scripture as a fundamental element.

British pride never had a more sincere mouthpiece than John Fletcher. He was fond of saying that he was a republican by birth, but British by choice.[7] Again he frequently alluded to 'this favourite Isle'.[8] Once he went so far as to apostrophize thus: England—'Thou centre of the civilized world, where Reformed Christianity, deep thinking wisdom and polite learning, with all its refinements have fixed their abode'.[9] It was not in the first

[2] E.g. *Works*, V.235. [3] E.g. ibid. VII.325. [4] E.g. ibid. p. 323.
[5] E.g. ibid. p. 5. [6] E.g. ibid. VII.369. [7] E.g. ibid. pp. 18, 40.
[8] E.g. ibid. IV.25. [9] Ibid. II.88.

flush of enthusiasm that he wrote that, but after wrestling with drink, gambling, rough sports, obscenity, immorality, blasphemy and a good deal more for twelve years.

Here was a parish priest who was in notable contrast with his predecessor and with neighbouring clergy for miles around. 'He's a Methodist' was the general shriek. Fletcher never repudiated it, never hedged, never mitigated it. He admitted it even in print.[10] Why? Because he believed that essentially it was the religion of the Church of England Fathers.

Let us now ask what this Anglican-Methodist Ministry meant in the actual life of the parish. First as to its innovations, or what seemed to be such. The common objection to his ministry, says Fletcher, was that it carried religion too far. It was making far too serious a business of it. This term 'Seriousness', in fact, put the situation into a nutshell. It produced in practice a sharp division of parishioners into 'serious people' and others, so that before long the term 'parishioners' takes on a less religious meaning. This was not Fletcher's intention: indeed standing on the principle of a comprehensive Church (he was never tired of recalling the Baptismal Covenant) his efforts were calculated to make all his parishioners 'serious'. In fact, however, and inevitably it will seem to most people, the Methodists drew apart by drawing together. For them, so it would appear to the rest, Fletcher called into operation all the mechanism of Methodism—class- and band-meetings, Society meetings, preaching-stations, and at length Circuit and preachers' plan.

Behind the sifting process is Fletcher's doctrine of the Ministry, and behind that his doctrines of the Fall and Redemption. In a passage too long to quote, but which can be summarized, he sets forth the grand business of the ministry as to rouse, to warn, to probe, to amputate, and

[10] E.g. ibid. VII.p. 406.

to heal.[11] He does this in the first instance by open-air preaching and by visiting. The latter should not have been an innovation, of course, but undertaken with thoroughness and with so serious intention, it might have seemed such. The novelty about open-air preaching was to find the vicar thus demeaning himself. Open-air preaching, necessarily extempore, on the occasion of funerals was in all probability really an innovation in Madeley. Many burials took place on Sundays from economic necessity. Big crowds usually gathered. Fletcher was ever an evangelical opportunist, and he improved the occasions with a fervent address on man's mortality and Christ's immortality.

Soon there followed an intensification of what may properly be called 'Prayer Book Religion'. When this book was taken at its minimum, Fletcher was roused into utterances of biting irony. Of minimum-religion parsons he wrote: 'If a tolerable part of his unclean flock do but disguise themselves three or four times in a year for the purpose of making their appearance at the sacramental table, he is perfectly satisfied with the good order of his parish; especially when the most detestable vices such as extortion, theft, adultery, or murder are not openly practised in it. This outward kind of decency which is so satisfactory to the worldly minister, and which is ordinarily affected by the constraining force of the civil laws, rather than by the truths of the gospel, affords the faithful pastor but little consolation.'[12]

In all Fletcher's *Works* there is scarcely a single complimentary reference to his fellow-clergy. 'Like Priest, like People' he sighed many times. Here he placed the blame for what he called 'the dying embers of grace in the Church'. He admired Wesley most of all because God had made him 'the first and principal instrument in the late revival of internal religion in our Church'.[13]

[11] *Works*, II.143.   [12] Ibid. VIII.112.   [13] Ibid. II.310.

SAINT

That Fletcher was overdoing things was the common topic of conversation. There is a passage in the *Equal Check* wherein we hear an echo from the public house. Fletcher writes of those who say, 'For their part they see no need of so many sermons, lectures and Sacraments in the Church; no need of so much singing, reading, praying and godly conversation in private houses; no need of such strictness in keeping the Sabbath holy, etc.'[14]

Such a passage makes clear what were the main lines of Fletcher's renovation of Church life. Sermons as distinct from lectures, relate to Sunday worship. It is not possible to be absolutely certain what was the Sunday tradition at Madeley when he became vicar, as no register of services has come to light. It is certain that Fletcher did something new by preaching at Evensong. He catechized according to the rubric every Sunday in the Service of Evensong, but whether that was novel too, we cannot say. Probably there was innovation only in its being regular. The sermon at Evensong was gratuitous. Years later Fletcher warns his curate, Greaves, against going beyond his strength and reminds him that 'the evening sermon is not part of our *stated* duty'.[15] In 1775 Fletcher is still preaching twice a Sunday at Madeley.[16]

At which morning service was there a sermon? The reference to 'stated duty' of preaching each Sunday can relate only to the Communion Office, for only there is a Sermon ordered. Whether Fletcher anticipated the modern 'Sung Eucharist' by having hymns and sermon at Communion, we cannot be sure. Casual remarks in his writings point to 'the Prayers', i.e. 'Matins', being said each Sunday.[17] Similarly with the Litany. Allusions to the danger of glib repetition of the Nicene Creed every Lord's day,[18] along with the tittle-tattle about 'so many Sacraments' make it fairly certain that Fletcher had a

[14] *Works*, IV.75. [15] Fletcher's italics. [16] Tyerman, p. 333.
[17] E.g. *Works*, III.313. [18] Ibid. II.140.

weekly celebration. There is presumptive evidence that he observed the rubrics about Holy Communion on the Red Letter Days also.

'Lectures' were sermons or ethical addresses, usually delivered verbatim from print or manuscript, in a consecrated building, and usually unrelated to the Offices of Public Worship. Fletcher had only been at Madeley one month when he introduced week-evening preaching in the Church, thus turning a custom which was mainly but not entirely academic and metropolitan, to country uses. In a letter to Lady Huntingdon he says that he intends to preach with his sermon-case only in his hand. The phrase 'sermon-case only' might mean that Fletcher was not taking a written sermon—but only an outline. But the phrase conceals a fact which renders this appearance of novelty a thoroughly Anglican practice. The fact is that inside the covers were liturgical prayers and the Bidding Prayer prescribed by Canon 55, to be used by all Preachers before all sermons, lectures and homilies. Wesley himself drew a distinction between the Methodist preaching-service and the statutory services of the Church. The Methodist service, he says, presupposes public prayer. In this respect it is akin to University Sermon and Bidding Prayer.[19] Such preaching is allowed by the Church of England as supplementary to Sunday preaching, which is exactly how Fletcher used it.

As time went on Fletcher was led from novelty and innovation into irregularities. His plea that Methodism was the Church of England recovering her pristine glory, struck Church of England men as quite inconsistent with his invasion of neighbouring parishes to support what seemed like conventicles. His most compelling defence was not to Fathers or precedents, but empirical, in such heart-rending outbursts as this—'When brutish ignorance and heathenish wickedness break out into such unnatural

[19] *The Works of John Wesley* (1829-31) VIII.321.

enormities, who would not break through the hedge of canonical regularity?'[20] Thus once again we are led back to his conception of Ministry. The spirit of academical pursuits is far removed from such passages as the following: 'If in a parish that is unhappy enough to have a pastor of this kind [worldly and insincere] a few persons are happily converted to God and united together in Jesus Christ; if, having one heart and one soul they frequently join together in prayer and praise, mutually exhorting and provoking one another to love and good works;—the worldly minister, instantly alarmed, imagines that these persons, for the sake of forming a new sect are destroying the unity of the Church; when, on the contrary they are but just about to experience *the communion of the saints*. And if he be possessed of zeal and party-spirit he will labour to make it appear that these Christians who are beginning to love as brethren, are forming conventicles to disturb the order both of Church and State. Such a minister will give encouragement to companies of jugglers, dancers, and drunkards, rather than tolerate a society which has *Christian charity* for its object and basis.'[21]

Unquestionably Fletcher had the intrinsic moral and spiritual right to put his finger on this fundamental sore of his Church as will be seen if we look particularly at his own work as Pastor, Priest and Preacher.

V. PASTOR

All who knew Fletcher were struck by the largeness of his pastoral heart—by what is sometimes called his 'love of souls'. This aspect of his ministry has been more thoroughly explored than any other. The stories of his ministry in plague-infested houses, his charity in kind and money to the poverty stricken, his individual encounters with cursing, swearing, blaspheming, gaming, gambling, cruel and lustful parishioners, have been told many

[20] *Works*, II.95. [21] Ibid., VIII.267.

times. His courage in the presence of bull-baiting mobs, his prophetic denunciations at the Wakes, his tramps around the hamlets at sunrise on Sunday mornings waking up his people for church with a clanging handbell—these things are well known. Some readers will recall his care for children, and particularly his own provision of parochial day- and Sunday-schools.

Such pastoral concern was not typical of the clergy of his time: it characterized Methodism. But Fletcher insisted that this pastoral heart was not out of place in the Anglican body. All, or almost all that seemed to distinguish the Methodist conception of Ministry (thinking of the ordained ministry at the moment) Fletcher finds in the Anglican Standards. Concerning the 'Call' for instance, he wrote: 'I think the desire of being stiled Reverend or Right Reverend, and the prospect of a living or a mitre are very improper motives for assuming the sacred character. And I am such an enthusiast as to believe our Church in the right for requiring that all her ministers should not only be called but even MOVED by the Holy Ghost to take the office of Ambassadors for Christ upon themselves'.[22]

No enthusiastic doctrine of Ministry could go farther, in Fletcher's view, than a Bishop's charge at the Ordination of a Priest: 'See that you never cease your labour, care and diligence until you have done all that lieth in you, to bring all such as shall be committed to your charge into that agreement of faith and that ripeness and perfectness of age in Christ, that there be no place left among you for error in religion, or viciousness in life.'[23]

In the fulfilment of that ideal Fletcher used what are known as the 'Occasional Offices' of the Book of Common Prayer with no sense of restriction. The great pastoral opportunities—emergency baptism, churching of women, sickness, life's last hours, and the like, he took with

[22] *Works*, VII.339.   [23] Ibid. VI.161, and elsewhere.

Prayer Book seriousness and with Methodist intensity. Celebrations of Holy Communion were not thought frightening in the homes of his sick parishioners.

The Methodist provision of class, society and prayer-meeting was supplemental to the Prayer Book. If Fletcher failed at all, it was just here: Wesley thought that Fletcher's Methodist discipline left something to be desired. It is probable that Fletcher had his hands full, and so trusted the Societies and groups to exercise their own discipline by agreement.[24]

In the matter of visiting, Fletcher was impeccable. He once wrote concerning regular visitation: 'The most powerful nerve of the sacred ministry is ecclesiastical discipline.'[25] He was known in every house, and so was that 'Helvetic bluntness'. Each visit was a challenge to the lapsed, an instruction to the children and a prayerful encouragement to the faithful to press on to perfection.[26]

Wherever the pastor was he bore his parishioners—all of them—before God in prayer.[27] His greatest energies were for the least deserving. 'The more sterile the soil appears which he is called upon to cultivate,' he wrote, 'the more he waters it both with his tears and with the sweat of his brow; the more he implores for it the dew of heaven and the influences of that divine Sun which spreads light and life through every part of the Church.'[28] What he could not do by his presence he did by pastoral letter—but we shall consider this subject in the chapter which deals with Fletcher as a writer.

VI. PRIEST

Protestant though he was Fletcher did not demur at being called a 'parish priest',[29] nor did he think that the sacerdotal functions of the priesthood could be assumed

---

[24] Cf. ibid. V.337.   [25] Ibid. VIII.166.
[26] See Cox's *Life of Fletcher*, pp. 50-3.   [27] Cf. *Works*, VII.460.
[28] Ibid. VIII.115.   [29] Ibid. IV.88.

by the unordained. If occasionally, like Wesley, he tilts at the folly of arguing about ecclesiastical garments instead of doing battle with the devil, this does not mean that these things have no value. There is no easy-going 'low churchmanship' in Fletcher. Neither is there any spiky high-churchmanship. If one has to use these cloudy terms we would have to say that he was an 'Evangelical High Churchman'. We shall take a look at his 'evangelicalism' in Chapter Four. At this point we view his priesthood in relation to the Liturgy.

Fletcher's admiration for the Liturgy matches that which he had for the Constitution. By Liturgy, of course, Fletcher meant the whole of the 1662 Book of Common Prayer. There is not the least indication that he was dissatisfied with any part of it, except the damnatory clauses of the Athanasian Creed. Even about these he would go no farther than to say that he would never use them without explanation. When someone remarked that his Subscription precluded this he replied by urging the more hopeful New Testament attitudes to the good pagan, and argued thus: 'If these two creeds are irreconcilable, I think it more reasonable that Athanasius should bow to Peter warmed by the spirit of love; than that Peter should bow to Athanasius heated by controversial opposition.'[30]

The Quakers were stirred by Fletcher's defence of formal prayer, and some of his Methodist friends were uneasy at his loyalty to it. Some Free Churchmen who admire the spontaneity of his spiritual life and the apostolic freedom of his preaching, wonder at his submission to a restrained liturgy. There is a connection between these, however, which is understood only by those well versed in the spiritual life. Fletcher frequently fell back upon what he called 'our excellent liturgy'.[31] Scores of quotations from all the Offices are given as 'the

[30] *Works*, IV.263.   [31] E.g. ibid. VII.370.

testimony of our own excellent Church'.[32] He defends the liturgical use of the Lord's Prayer, believing it to be purposeful in every Prayer Book Service.[33] In particular he commends the 'reasonable simplicity' of the Communion Office.[34] The truth and order of the Liturgy appealed to him.[35] Few Anglican Clergymen today are so happy as to believe that their Church is 'everywhere consistent with itself and with the Scripture' even along a narrow line of reasoning.[36]

Formal, thoughtless repetition is never far from religious utterance. Fletcher often warned his congregation of its dangers and frequently charged them with it.[37] But it never occurred to him as a solution that 'free' or 'extempore' prayer should displace the ordered forms.

Liturgy is mainly utterance, as far as Fletcher was concerned. If he thought of 'action' at all, it was as of something quite subservient. His view of the Liturgy properly speaking, i.e. the Office of Holy Communion, is not that it is primarily an offering to God, except in the sense in which all prayer is offered, but that it is a means of attaining Christian Perfection.[38] The aesthetic appeal of things Anglican, most people would say, was *almost* lost upon him. But the qualification may mean more than appears at first sight. For instance, his respect for the architectural setting of the liturgy is apparent to those who know how the Church's terminology is used. There is significance in references to 'desk', 'pulpit', 'chancel', 'ornaments', 'bell', and so on. These were, he knew, part of the Anglican appeal to worship and the good life.[39] The 'desk', for example, is not a thing of convenience, but a piece of church furniture distinguished deliberately from the pulpit as the place where the prayer of the Daily Office was wont to be made.[40] Again, the Chancel is

[32] E.g. ibid. II.248-9.   [33] Ibid. p. 156.   [34] Ibid. II.248.
[35] Ibid. VIII.302.   [36] Ibid. II.18.   [37] E.g. ibid. II.140.
[38] Ibid. VI.158.   [39] Ibid. VII.234.   [40] Cf. ibid. II.383.

associated with the Commandments, which means, of course, with the whole Communion Office.[41]

The phrase 'Daily Office' has smacked of high-churchmanship to low and latitudinarian churchmen. Fletcher not infrequently uses the phrase. It is very probable that he said Matins and Evensong in his church every day. In one place he speaks of the Church's daily prayer in the *Te Deum* for sinless purity.[42] On 30th January 1767 (a Friday) he alludes to the set Old Testament lesson.[43] Actually that day was kept in Fletcher's time as a day of fasting to commemorate the murder of Charles I. It is not likely that he would single that day out: rather he would observe the Church Calendar, keeping the Feasts, and using the Propers.

Fletcher's use of the liturgy to prove doctrine might be unwelcome to liturgiologists and aesthetes, but it was absolutely sound. He did so on a big scale. He was sure of the 'Anglican Suffrage'. He was never happier than when standing four-square upon Scripture, Homilies, Liturgy and the Articles.[44]

Often, in reading Fletcher's writings, one comes across phraseology which suggests the Tractarian Movement—such things as 'Fasting', 'standing to our baptismal vow', etc. If anyone would be at pains to gather together all his references to Baptism, to mention only that, it would soon become plain how unsatisfactory it is simply to call Fletcher a 'great evangelical'.

VII. PREACHER

In his lifetime Fletcher was celebrated more as a preacher than as a writer. One who knew him well said: 'I would rather have heard one sermon from Mr Fletcher *viva voce* than have read a volume of his works. . . . His preaching was apostolic; while his writings, though enlightened, are

[41] Cf. *Works*, IV.334. [42] Ibid. VI.155. [43] Ibid. VII.425.
[44] E.g. ibid. V.19.

but human.'[45] 'Apostolic' is also Lady Huntingdon's description of his preaching at the time when he had been at Madeley five years. And those who have written about him just after his death and since, can find no better term to express his pulpit demeanour, delivery and message.

His natural vivacity was so obvious that an extempore style was expected of him. In his earliest attempts in English there were sighs, gaps, hesitations and interjected prayers. At Madeley, he had a manuscript at first, but became more and more extempore. Scores of little four-page outlines are preserved: they give not the slightest indication of how he preached.

It is instructive to notice both his homiletic precepts and practices and to compare them. His ideal of Preaching, as of so much else, is to be found in his *Portrait of St Paul*, a document which might well replace Wesley's *Notes* as a Methodist Preacher's Standard. The chief object of preaching, Fletcher states, is Conversion. The parish system, for all its usefulness, cannot justify a conversionless ministry. In effect he says: 'Convert—or move on.' True, he demands patient and persistent trial before the closure is put.[46]

Apostolic preaching is urgent, simple, direct.[47] It is diagnosis of human misery, warning of danger, and application of the Christian remedy with gospel realism. Congregations are to be 'shaken' (a favourite Wesley word this) to good purpose. Fletcher summarizes this in the excellent counsel which Luther gave to Melanchthon: 'So preach that those who do not fall out with their sins may fall out with thee.'[48]

Such preaching is the very opposite of popular preaching: it will almost certainly lead to smaller congregations. Still, this is but part of the good pastor's duty. He must

[45] Cox, *Life of Fletcher*, p. 39.　　[46] *Works*, VIII.115.
[47] Ibid. pp. 163ff.　　[48] Ibid. II.386.

preach the tenderness of God also, addressing his brethren with the utmost affection and regard.[49] This ministry of wounding and healing finds neat expression thus: 'The preaching of the true minister is that through which God employs his power for the conversion of sinners and the edification of believers.'[50]

Some of Fletcher's views on preaching are delightfully naïve. For instance, he argues that there was no oratory in Christ or the apostles. None of them wrote sermons. Neither, he says, is there any account that their successors were instructed to write and deliver their sermons like public orators.[51]

The average country parish in the eighteenth century had all too little preaching. Very few clergy prepared a polished sermon. Only in some Continental churches and in fashionable town churches in England were there 'weekly exercises of learning and art'.[52]

Why did he object to the written sermon, as such, when he used the Homilies himself—and quoted copiously from them? With childlike simplicity he says that when our neighbour's house is on fire we need no document to help us give a warning. Yet he borrowed 'the plain, nervous language of the Homilies'.[53]

His judgement failed him when he set down that when once 'approved' sermons are written they could be delivered by trained schoolboys.[54] It seems not to have occurred to him that art in the Liturgy might fittingly be matched with art in the Sermon, and that his argument would tell against the Liturgy also. Yet in pleading for a virile pulpit ministry within the 'incomparable Liturgy' he was, many will agree, as near to the ideal as it is possible to come.

After all, it is not art but 'mere oratory' which Fletcher condemns. For equally he despises those preachers who

[49] *Works*, VIII.79.   [50] Ibid. p. 178.   [51] Ibid. VIII.163.
[52] Ibid. p. 166.   [53] E.g. ibid. III.154.   [54] Ibid. VIII.167.

'conscious of their own ability . . . make little or no preparation for one of the most solemn duties that can possibly be discharged'. Study and homiletic skill can be aids to an evangelical ministry.[55]

If Fletcher was able to discern the secret of his own preaching—and there is doubt about that—he was unable to communicate it. It had the stamp of inspiration upon it. He was enwrapt in the task with the utmost concentration whilst he preached, but afterwards, quite often, he could not even recall his text.[56]

There is an art which conceals art, and there is an artlessness which excels art. Doubtless he improved his talent, but the more satisfactory explanation is that he was born to it.

When he chose he could write an oratorical sermon. If he preached the one on 'The Dreadful Phenomenon' at all as he wrote it, it must have been wonderful simply as an utterance. Such utterance casts its spell over men. And it is paradoxical that in his case 'apostolic preaching' was 'popular', in that he filled his Church to breaking-point.

[55] Ibid. p. 170.   [56] Cf. Ibid. VIII.80.

CHAPTER THREE

Literary Vocation

I. SOME LITERARY NOTICES

FLETCHER's biographer, Tyerman, more with painstaking industry than imagination, leads his readers slowly through the labyrinth of the Calvinistic Controversy. Lengthy quotations are justified in an apologetic way. Tyerman himself gets tired, and almost expects his readers to feel weary. He acknowledges that some of Fletcher's writing is out of date, dry and tedious, and that its chief value is as a witness to Fletcher's industry and humble-mindedness. But Tyerman is staunch in his loyalty to the *Checks to Antinomianism*, particularly to the last of these containing Fletcher's account of Perfection—a treatise 'invaluable' and 'never equalled'.

Another Methodist, The Reverend J. Marrat, writing in 1902, expressed the view that Fletcher's *Works* 'are worthy of a better place than the shelf in the library used only for obsolete works. They constitute a literature in which there is much that is unique, curious and beautiful. There are evidences of wide outlooks on theology and various aspects of human life and full understanding of the tendencies of the times, whether in the direction of scepticism or on the lines of what was then regarded as strict orthodoxy. From a level strain there are many ascents to a lofty and impassioned eloquence, not inferior to the finest achievements of writers recognized as classical.'

Alongside these estimates from within Methodism may be set that of Cox the Vicar of Bridgnorth in Shropshire, written in 1822. After enumerating Fletcher's defects as 'exuberant diffuseness' and 'national floridness' (this might refer to his French rather than to his Swiss heritage) and (in letters) religious preciousness, Cox continues: 'The whole of his other publications manifest a degree of elegance, force and correctness of expression which could hardly have been expected from a foreigner. His imagination is always lively, his descriptions animated, his illustrations uncommonly happy; and his reasoning acute, clear and convincing.' In Cox's view Fletcher had the abilities to 'have occupied no inconsiderable rank either as a humorist, a poet, or an impassioned writer'. Fletcher is generally remembered as fulfilling only the last of these roles. Yet there is much to be said in support of Cox's claim, and the attempt to do so is made in this chapter. Our object will be to sketch Fletcher's literary activities and to analyse his style of writing, in the hope that those who are interested in the communication of religion in group, or homiletically, may take down Fletcher's volumes from their forlorn security in the large libraries.

II. LITERARY ROLES

(1) *Poet*

Who can say whether and what Fletcher would have written had he not been an Anglican clergyman caught up in the toils of a sweeping religious revival? There are those who believe he had the soul of a poet. Charles Hiatt, a Shropshire man writing on the literary associations of his county, reckons Fletcher as a fanatic, rating his literary significance much below that of Baxter, but avers that his most interesting production was a poem in French. The work referred to was written in Switzerland about 1777, and it appeared in England in an enlarged form in the year Fletcher died. Tyerman calls it a remarkable production springing out of true poetic fire. The fact remains that this poem, which was translated into English with the title *Grace and Nature*, is uncharacteristic of Fletcher. It is not included in Benson's edition of the *Works*. The best that can be said for it as a poem is that it reaches the level of Young's *Night Thoughts*, and indeed it reminds us of that work.

(2) *Letter Writer*

It is not as poet but as pastor that we touch Fletcher's characteristic literary activity. Many of his letters have been preserved. They are truly spiritual. Whereas Wesley's correspondence is full of the practical business of the Connexion, Fletcher rarely mentions day-to-day events. His main concern is with personal holiness rather than with social religion. We find, indeed, references to gifts of wine, cheese, cloth and other commodities, but it is as pegs upon which to hang some instruction in evangelical truth. There is no humour, no playfulness, hardly a smile. Unwittingly the letters afford glimpses into parish life or provide sidelights upon aspects of the Revival.

The letters fall into two groups—those to individuals, and those to his parishioners at Madeley. The style is the same throughout, as indeed it is throughout all his works, except that the vocabulary in the letters is simpler and free from the technicalities of theology.

In Benson's edition a good many of Fletcher's letters are to be found in the biographical setting in the first volume. The rest are grouped together in Volume VII under the heading 'Pastoral and Familiar Letters'.

Amongst Fletcher's correspondents were persons of wealth and title, Anglican clergymen including the Wesley brothers, Nonconformist and Methodist preachers, and individual parishioners at Madeley.

To all these Fletcher wrote with great courtesy but with firmness. The letters make up a little body of practical spiritual teaching to which we turn again in Chapter Five. Here our concern is with their literary style. They reveal all the characteristic features—deep seriousness of tone, the hopeful note, the staccato phrases in the imperative mood, striking facility in manipulating Scripture idiom, colloquial expressions, neat aphoristic sentences, allegory, quaint illustration and allusion, and at times a whimsical humility. As the main lines of our study in this chapter will be to examine these and similar things, there is no need to particularize with respect to the letters.

The motive for writing the letters lay at the very centre of his life. He states it with great simplicity in one letter written in 1775—'I find myself drawn by friendship and pastoral care to send you a few lines'.[1] Fletcher never begrudged this part of his literary work as he did a good deal of his controversial writing.

(3) *Controversialist*

A sense of sacred duty held Fletcher to long spells of controversial writing. But he knew, as Wesley once said, that controversy was a field in which it is easier to lose love than to find truth. Almost every critic testifies that Fletcher showed invincible patience and courtesy towards his opponents. But, duty or not, controversy was to Fletcher a quagmire, out of which he only slowly climbed. He often sighed: 'My controversy weighs upon my hands: but I must go through with it.'

On the other hand there is a fine passage in *The Fictitious and Genuine Creed* which sets out Fletcher's gains and which forms a first-rate practical apology for close, if irksome, ministerial study.[2] To one of his intimate friends he spoke of this literary activity as 'scribbling in the mornings'. He justified it laconically with the remark that 'a man must do something, and I may as well investigate truth as do anything else, except solemn praying and visiting my flock'. In the same context he suggests that he would sooner preach than write, but as he is

[1] *Works*, VII.440.   [2] Ibid. III.461-3.

limited by throat-trouble, he is compelled to write more than he likes.[3]

Neither the theology nor the history of the Controversy is of importance to our approach to its literature as literature, but a few facts are necessary if the reader is to know what it is he is being asked to study. There came a point in Wesley's ministry (in the year 1770) when he realized acutely that undue emphasis upon the divine side of Christianity could and did in fact often result in under-emphasis of its moral aspects. When this form of religion became unbalanced it resulted in delusion, and even sheltered immorality beneath its skirts. As we would put it, a religion which is too mental and too emotional is not practical enough. At root, the question is the age-old one about 'Faith' and 'Works'. The Calvinists turned the question into a dilemma and said that to make salvation a matter of merit is to denude faith, and to dishonour Christ, and to dethrone God. The Arminians maintained that Christ is Christ, and God is God, even though man as a free-willing being can only be saved in the formation of character. Fundamental in this salvation is man's moral image as taught in Scripture. On this foundation stands the full Christian image to which Wesley gives the name Christian Perfection.

It was in defence of Wesley that Fletcher began to write. As feelings were stirred, he found himself dealing with publications by the Hill brothers, Sellon, Toplady, Caleb Evans and others. Later on he championed Trinitarian Theology against the Deists and the Humanists. In a period of five and a half years from the middle of 1771, he produced practically the whole bulk of his writings, that is to say, work running at least to the extent of five octavo volumes of over four hundred pages each, closely printed.

The modern reader is apt to be confused by Fletcher's

[3] *Works*, I.176-8.

titles, sub-titles and divisions into 'Parts'. The title-pages in the Benson edition of the *Collected Works*, are explicable though not at a glance, but the printing of different Roman numerals on opposite pages complicates matters further. For instance in Volume IV, pp. 296-7, we have *Equal Check*, Part II, indicated on the left-hand page, and *Scripture Scales*, Part I, on the right-hand page. The title-page (271) reveals that *Scripture Scales*, Part I, is a sub-heading of *Equal Check*, Part II.

The titles themselves are unattractive to the modern reader. There are six '*Checks to Antinomianism*'. It should be remembered that the term 'Antinomian' had a sting in Fletcher's day, and that the phrase 'give a check to' was part of common speech and that it carried the kind of tone which often attaches to our expression—'I'll put a stop to that'. Titles such as *Scripture Scales*, above mentioned, may have a quaint sound, but they are not intriguing. Nearly all Fletcher's titles indicate polemics. Several compositions invade the field of politics, and one or two deal with philosophical and ethical issues.

The very last thing to do with Fletcher is to wade through the *Collected Works*. Fletcher himself thought that his *Scripture Scales* was more valuable than much of his other work. But it was not so. This bit of inspired hackwork could be put alongside say Anthony of Padua's *Moral Concordances*, but its influence was far less than that of the *Checks*, which have been meat and drink to many evangelical Christians who know little or nothing of their origin in controversy.

The general reader might start by looking into *The Appeal to Matter of Fact and Common Sense*. It was written in 1772, and in some ways it is the most liberal of all Fletcher's compositions. Descriptive passages in the fashion of the times are to be found there.[4] The work contains many references to the poet Young, several to Milton, besides

[4] Ibid. II.20ff.

allusions to classical writers and contemporary philosophers. This work manifests a most extensive vocabulary and a wealth of idiomatic expressions. In addition there is an abundance of that sort of language which is often called poetic—words, for instance, such as 'adamantine', 'balmy', 'melancholy', 'ravishing', as well as a quantity of literary stock-in-trade—'deceitful morasses', 'faithless quicksands', 'festal board', 'romantic prospect', 'smiling landscape' and such like. Interwoven with these is the language of everyday life—some of it 'low' and even vulgar to hypersensitive ears—'bedlamites', 'blockhead', 'brazen-faced', 'brood', 'cry down', 'fool's coat', 'infernal crew'. Here may be seen hard-worked adjectives such as 'complicated', 'execrable' and 'meridian', as well as rarer terms such as 'afflictive', 'appetance', 'condign', 'consentaneous', 'decollation', 'diastole', 'metamorphoze', 'systole', and many others. The *Appeal* is in fact a quite typical and interesting specimen of Fletcher's literary work, and in addition to forming an introduction to the aspects of his style just mentioned, it displays his allegorizing skill, his knowledge of proverbial lore, his acquaintance with rhetoric, and his fondness of novel word-combinations.

Candidates for Holy Orders could do a great deal worse than study his *Portrait of St Paul*, not for its objective scholarship, but for its idealization of the pastoral office. This was written far from his parish (in Switzerland, to be exact), but he has that parish very much in mind throughout.

Those whose chief concern is evangelical, might well start by reading the *Address to Earnest Seekers of Salvation* which forms an appendix to the *Appeal* previously mentioned. Here is to be found a simple product with no sign of novelty, but containing a passionate recital of gospel theology. Most noticeable is the massive use of Scripture as quotation, but more remarkably, as dialogue. Here

SAINT

the reader will see a man thinking, dreaming, imagining and creating—all with the material of the Bible. It comes as a shock to find Christ uttering words of Old Testament narrative and phraseology from the Litany in the Book of Common Prayer.[5] The *Address* sounds the note of warning. 'Flee', it cries. To whom? Here comes the gospel invitation. The alarm and the refuge are pressed upon the reader so that he can hardly help feeling that Christ is speaking, and speaking to him.[6]

III. LITERARY STYLE

We turn now to examine Fletcher's style of writing. The subject has not engaged much serious attention. It has, however, unsuspected ramifications, which might well run into a volume given over to it completely.

Fletcher disclaimed learning. He justified his *Vindication of the Catholic Faith* as being intended for 'persons' of all ranks and capacities not for the learned.[7] He believed that the Revival did not gain much from his pen. This modesty was typical, but it is no guide whatever to the formation of a sound literary judgement of Fletcher's works, however truly it reflects his own feelings.

It must be apparent to any one familiar with eighteenth-century religious writing, that Fletcher's style is very English. No one would know, from his style alone, that English was not his mother tongue. Very rarely he recalls the fact that he has had to adopt English and recognize the possibility that it may have niceties which escape him.[8] Within the corpus of his *Works* items of self-criticism can be found. Writing in 1774, for instance, he reflects: 'In endeavouring to render my style nervous I have sometimes rendered it provoking.'[9] But the two illustrations there given of expressions which he would soften, i.e. 'absolutely graceless' into 'devoid of grace', and

---

[5] *Works*, II.203-5.   [6] Ibid. II.196-7.   [7] Ibid. IX.16.
[8] E.g. ibid. III.153.   [9] Ibid. p. 464.

'reprobated culprits' into 'those . . . reprobated' are not convincing evidence that Fletcher was guilty of the fault of impropriety. There is a startling honesty about Fletcher's wordmanship, as we shall see. No—Wesley on Fletcher is preferable to Fletcher on himself. Comparing Fletcher with Whitefield, Wesley wrote: 'He had a richer flow of fancy, a stronger understanding, a far greater treasure of learning both in languages, philosophy, philology and divinity.'[10]

(1) *Vocabulary*

So far as the present writer is aware, no one has followed Wesley's clue about Fletcher's love of words. In broaching the subject, it is not to study it from the standpoint of comparative linguistics, but to make clear one incontrovertible fact, which is that Fletcher was a word-man who can stand beside any in his own day.

He had an immense vocabulary under wonderful control. The craze for trying to say everything in terms of one syllable has no support from this writer. Basic English would have reduced him to gibberish. Truth is so glorious, so profound, so spiritual that the maximum vocabulary is needed to embody it, to express it, to communicate it. At this point, perhaps more than anywhere else, we see how unreliable Fletcher's self-criticism is. He honestly believed he wrote for the common man; but the common man must often have boggled at the philological apparitions which Fletcher brought before his eyes. And many so-called educated men in Fletcher's day and in our own, must have found themselves in need of a dictionary to read him. We shall invoke the aid of the *Oxford English Dictionary*, using lists of words and references to open up the Fletcher mine, not only to the professional lexicographer, but to all who are interested in the communication of religion by means of language.

[10] *Works*, I.185.

(a) Fletcher's Memorial in the Oxford English Dictionary

The following terms are illustrated in the *O.E.D.* by Fletcher instances:

- Aspersed (ppl. adj.)
- Auto-da-fé
- † Condecency
- * Consentaneous
- † Covert
- Dally
- † Declarative
- Disburdened (ppl. adj.)
- Favonian
- Flagrant
- Foment
- * Halberd-bearer
- Hocus pocus
- Inadmissible
- Indecently
- * Iron-clay
- * Justiciar
- Mandrel (Miner's tool)
- * Out-kick
- † Out-sin
- Perfectively
- Plain-spoken
- † Pre-possessed (adj.)
- Remonstrant
- Seminally
- Solifidianism
- Stamina
- Suscitation
- Swiss
- Vapourer

This short list is not the result of a search through the *O.E.D.* Doubtless it is very incomplete—but it is an excellent introduction to our study. It contains five words (marked thus: *) which, according to present records, appear in Fletcher for the first time in English literature, either absolutely, or in a particular usage. Five terms (marked thus: †) occur in Fletcher at the latest date that has been recorded. In this little list appear industrial and military terms, an item or two of common speech, and technical terms of theology and ecclesiastical history. The majority would be unfamiliar to our friend the common man.

(b) Wordman Ahead of His Time

Still using the *O.E.D.* as our yardstick, we get a fresh insight into Fletcher's wordmanship when we realize how up-to-date (in some cases we might say before-the-date) he was. In the list next to be given Fletcher used the terms earlier than any other writer so far recorded. In most of the instances his priority is absolute: in several, e.g. in the case of 'pre-ordained', the *O.E.D.* treats the term as a subsidiary, and has probably not sought the earliest, but simply any good instance.

Word	*O.E.D.: First instance*	*Fletcher: Date*
Attainability	Coleridge 1810	*Works*, V.450 1777
Aqueous (geol.)	*Playfair* 1802	,, VII.187 1776
Commonness (in sense of plain, undistinguished)	Hunt 1820	,, VI.388 1775
Congressmen	(Supplement) *American Times* 1780	,, VII.207 1776
Consentaneous	Fletcher 1774	,, II.18 1772
Convulsionaries	*All Year Round* 1859 (In French Trans. 1741)	,, VIII.301 1773
Disconcertment	Howells 1866	,, V.162 1775
Fourth-wheel	Britain [on Watchmaking] 1844	,, III.403 1774
Free-Agency	Burke 1786	,, V.174 1775
Furrowing	Cowper 1791	,, II.34 1772
Goog (American punishment)	(Spelt Gouge) Grose 1785	,, VII.207 1776
Inspectress	Wolcot (P. Pindar) 1785	,, VII.400 1763
Introverted	Cowper 1781	,, VI.401 1775
Lacedemonians	(as adj.) 1780 (as sbst.) 1870	,, VII.30 1775
Militia-men	Hamilton 1780	,, I.197 1776
Mobbing	(ppl. adj.) 1842 (attrib.) 1781	Tyerman, 353 1776
Nadir	Walpole 1793	*Works*, V.109 1775
Necessitarian	Cowper 1798	,, V.390 1777
Necessitarianism	Froude 1854	,, V.398 1777
Newsman (seller of newspapers)	Charlotte Smith 1796	,, IV.289 1773
Nicolaitan (adj.)	Blunt 1874	,, III.266 1772
Noahic	Duncan 1845	,, V.346 1775
Pot-boilers (political)	Hitchens and Drew 1824	,, VII.31 1775
Pre-ordained (ppl. adj.)	Baden-Powell 1855	,, III.338 1772

Word	O.E.D.: First instance	Fletcher: Date	
Publication (work published and sold)	Johnson 1780	*Works*, VII.253	1773
Q.E.D.	(Under 'Q. 2', abbreviations) Moore 1878	,, VII.107	1775
Reprobater (cf. with spelling 'er', rare)	Noble 1806	,, VI.88	1776
Sacrament-Day	(Sacrament Sunday) Simeon 1796	,, V.63	1775
Satanic (infernal)	Holcroft 1793	,, V.380	1775
Self-painter	('Self'—prefix, 1. C.) Disraeli 1840	,, VI.217	1775
Undarkened (ppl. adj.)	Shelley 1818	,, V.435	1777
Undecreed (adv.)	Gregory 1898	,, V.161	1775
Unscripturally	Russel 1824	,, IX.289	c.1784
Voltairian (adj.)	Morley 1879	,, V.388	1777

(*c*) *Ransacking the Past*

Mere up-to-dateness did not content Fletcher. He resurrected terms which had slumbered in obsolescence, in some cases, according to the *O.E.D.*, for many years. Cynical criticism would condemn this feature of his style. Some critics might dismiss it as the sort of quaintness to be expected of a foreigner who had steeped himself in sixteenth- and seventeenth-century English divines. But the matter is not to be dismissed so easily. In all probability some of these terms were used in speech even if in a limited circle, and it is a question whether they should be classified as obsolete in the literary sense. No claim is made that the list following is complete, but only that it is representative. Each term in it is classified in the *O.E.D.* as obsolete.

Word	O.E.D.'s Last instance	Fletcher: Date
Appendages (appendix—literary)	Hobbes 1657	Works, IV.262 1774
Complimental (formal)	Anon. 1703	,, VI.325 1775
Declarative	Fletcher 1772	,, IV.69 1774
Deject (verb, trans.)	Mede 1638	,, VII.123 1775
Dogmatical (=dogmatic)	*Chambers Cycl.* 1717-51	,, I.182 1774
Fasting (verb, quasi trans.)	Etheridge 1668	,, II.423 1771
Fare-spoken	Markham 1625	,, IV.419 1774
Free-willing (adjectival)	Coverdale 1535	,, V.67 1775
Irrespectively (adverb)	South 1716	,, III.234 1772
Massing-priest	Jeanes 1656	,, VI.77 1776
Moveables (sbst.)	Creech 1682	,, VII.216 1773
Mud-walls (fig.—of human body)	*Devout Communicant* 1670	,, V.410 1777
Probatory (=proving)	Anon. 1656	,, VI.46 1776
Rebaptization	Bargrave 1623	,, VII.46 1776
Retortible	Barlow 1609	,, VI.75 1776
Suffragan (=deputy)	Walpole 1770	,, VIII.25 1778–81
Super-angelical	Baxter 1690	,, V.243 1775
Swing (sbst. = noose, Tyburn)	Abel 1697	,, VI.41 1776
Tantamount (sbst.)	Maxwell 1646	,, IV.156 1774
Unchristian (verb)	Talbert 1712	,, III.367 1774

(d) Terminology 'Current-Coin'—but little used

The terms next to be considered are not recorded by the lexicographers as obsolete, but they are rarely found in eighteenth-century literature, or perhaps we should say that they have not been discovered by the lexicographers. It will be observed that several items in the following list are biblical, one or two sound like everyday speech, and the rest have an academic or professional flavour. It will be noticed also that the Fletcher instances would bring the *O.E.D.'s* word-histories nearer to our time by nearly two hundred years in some cases, and by one hundred years in most.

Word	Latest O.E.D. instance	Fletcher: Date		
Accomplishers	H. More 1687	*Works*,	VI.70	1776
Birdlime (fig.)	Vanbrugh 1705	,,	I.197	1776
Cainish	H. More 1689	,,	V.169	1775
Capernaites	Milton 1641	,,	II.262	1776
Communicative (impersonal)	De Foe 1719	,,	VI.163	1775
Counter-poison	Philips 1678	,,	VI.278	1775
Electing (ppl. adj.)	Hickman 1674	,,	V.302	1775
Evidencing (ppl. adj.)	Dryden 1682	,,	III.369	1774
Forbiddings (? rare plural)	Cheyne 1740	,,	VII.374	1776
Fore-described	Sidney 1581	,,	IV.419	1774
Fore-typified	Chauncy 1693	,,	IV.419	1774
Judicable	H. Care 1688	,,	V.391	1777
Lymphatic (vessels)	Evelyn 1649	,,	IX.45	1784
Miscarrying (ppl. adj.)	Rutherford 1637	,,	VI.255	1775
Pelagianize	Hickman 1674	,,	V.240	1775
Petty-Officers (parochial)	Shakespeare 1603	,,	II.80	1772
Plaguing (ppl. adj.)	Shakespeare 1591	,,	VI.247	1775
Pre-possessed (adj.)	Fletcher 1774	,,	VI.277	1775
Prevented (ppl. adj.)	Bacon 1605	,,	IV.177	1774
Propless	Denis 1743	,,	VI.58	1776
Resolving (ppl. adj.)	J.S. (translator) 1758	,,	VI.372	1775
Self-contracted	H. More 1655–87	,,	VI.234	1775
Spurring (vbl. sbst.)	Hieron 1617	,,	VI.290	1775

To this list should be added the scores of words used by Fletcher which would render the *O.E.D.'s* entries much more satisfactory from the view-point of lexical history.

For instance, under the terms 'Disuniter' and 'Exceedable' no true literary instance has so far appeared, and the authorities offered are early dictionaries. Fletcher used the former word in 1784 (*Works*, IX.36), and the latter in 1776 (*Works*, VI.6). Again, occasionally the *O.E.D.* records a term without reference of any sort. Two such, 'Disbelieving' (ppl. adj.) and 'Preyings' (vbl. sbst.), are to be found in Fletcher, in *Works*, II.218 (1772), and *Works*, IV.306 (1774), respectively. Finally, under this heading it should be noticed that Fletcher used scores, even hundreds, of uncommon words which are given in the *O.E.D.* with big gaps in their literary histories, such, for instance, as these: chlamys (cloak), impugned (ppl. adj.), impulsory (adj.), infrustrable, permissively, traduction, and unforeknown.

(e) Creative Genius

Fletcher was not the sort of philologist conjured up by the picture of a blear-eyed dictionary-maker. He was completely unaware that he was making lexical history. His striking word-combinations, original usages, nonce-usages, and new words come easily off his pen. The ability to create new words (by this is meant here not forms only, but forms with a positive content) is one of the surest signs of a lively mind. The terms in the next list are in the absolute sense unrecorded in the *O.E.D.*

Term	*Classification/Comment*	*Fletcher: Date*	
Best-concerted	Adjectival compound	*Works*, VI.72	1776
Brain-plate	Ironical nonce comb. patterned on 'breast-plate'	,, III.300	1772
Crispianity	Nonce word punning 'Christianity' upon name of Dr Crisp	,, V.143	1775
Decagrammaton	? Nonce word patterned on tetragrammaton (recorded by *O.E.D.*)	,, II.261	1771

SAINT

Term	Classification/Comment	Fletcher: Date	
Effectuosity	Perhaps Toplady's term originally	Works, V.400	1777
Felonage	Fletcher's conscious creation	,, III.41	1776
Half-diameters	nonce comb. to denote idea of meeting-point of opposites	,, V.97	1775
Imperfectionists	Ironical retort to 'perfectionists'	,, VI.135	1775
Introgression	? Nonce word patterned on 'intromission'	,, V.397	1777
Omnivigilant	In quotation from Toplady	,, V.390	1777
Scale-bottoms	Cf. scale-pans	,, IV.282	1774
Self-determiners	Cf. self-determinist	,, V.418	1777

Innumerable are the cases where Fletcher takes established words and puts them to novel uses of connotation or grammar. Those in the following list are representative:

Term	Classification/Comment	Fletcher: Date	
Candid	Noun—unrecorded as such	Works, V.264	1775
Carding (card-playing)	? An unrecorded colloquialism	,, VIII.257	1778
Caressed	Adjective—unrecorded as such	,, II.409	1775
Decretist	Nonce-usage meaning 'One holding Calvin's Decrees'	,, VI.84	1776
Engrosser	Ironical = one professing to monopolize	,, VI.277	1775
Exemplifying	Ppl. adj.—unrecorded as such	,, IV.437	1774
Haling-lines	Patterned on haling-way, etc.	,, V.178	1774
High-fed	Adjectival—cf. high-feeder	,, III.85	1772
Highway-money	? An unrecorded colloquialism, cf. highway-tax	,, VII.28	1776

Term	Classification/Comment	Fletcher: Date	
Limbus	Ironical, extended usage applied to a region of heaven	Works, III.40	1772
Mattering	Unrecorded as participle	,, IV.113	1774
Nabob-trade	Unrecorded combination	,, VII.180	1776
Non-voters	Unrecorded combination	,, VII.155	1776
Observatory	Distinctive figurative use	,, VIII.196	1778
Omnipotents (humans)	Unrecorded, except absolutely of the Deity	,, IV.16	1774
Pelagianistically	Fletcher parenthesizes 'if I may use the expression'. Not recorded as adverb	,, V.240	1775
Perfecting	Unrecorded as adjective	,, VI.390	1775
Ship-breakers	Patterned upon 'house-breakers'. Unrecorded cf. 'ship-breaking' (crime), dated only 1931	,, VII.119	1775
Solifidianizing	No verbal form recorded	,, VI.304	1775
Underminded	? Nonce form of 'undermined'	,, VII.264	1773
Vouchsafing	Participial forms not recorded	,, IX.265	1784

Obviously, a style overloaded with rarities and novelties would be intolerable. Fletcher was never charged with being unreadable. He keeps a balance between the technical language of the Academy, the stately language of the Church, and the language of everyday life.

(2) *English Idiom*
For a foreigner, Fletcher had a remarkable familiarity with the English way of thinking and speaking. In his day traditional forms, many of them corporal and robust and full of 'horse-sense', were common to all classes of society, and were not at all self-conscious. Take the case

SAINT

of proverbial expressions, for example. These are very plentiful in Fletcher. If he did not know as many as Wesley, he runs him a good second. They are present in all Fletcher's writings, witness the little selection of typical instances which follows:

Now or never	*Works*, I.120
Build castles in air	,, II.59
Blind as a beetle	,, III.37
All that glitters is not gold	,, IV.300
Leave no stone unturned	,, V.70
A burnt child dreads the fire	,, VI.283
A fool's paradise	,, VII.51
To err is the lot of humanity	,, VIII.50

Some of these, and others like them, occur not once only but often.

Only those who have studied the literary history of proverbs realize the difficulty of illustrating *from literature* some of the commonest expressions of *spoken* English. The present state of Proverb Lexicography as manifested in the *Oxford Dictionary of English Proverbs* (second edition) indicates this fact. A further revision is needed. With the two-fold object of suggesting Fletcher's usefulness in such revision, and of illustrating further the idiomatic element in his prose, attention is here drawn to a few specific items in his writings:

The Expression	*O.D.E.P.'s instance(s)*	*Fletcher: Date*		
Die in harness	None prior to Marryat, 1834	*Works*, I.197	1776
It is best to be on the safer side	None before Lean, 1902–1904	,,	VII.80	1776
Gild the pill	No literary instance— only collections of Proverbs	,,	VII.111	1776
Nature will be nature	None after Draxe, 1616	,,	VI.291	1775
Make scourge for own backs	None after Baxter, 1650	,,	II.42	1772

The Expression	O.D.E.P.'s instance(s)	Fletcher: Date	
Take care of the breed	No true literary instance prior to 1919	Works, II.130	1772
Falling out of lovers is the renewal of love [Latin]	No instance after Richardson, 1753	„ II.370	1771
The motto I thought myself obliged to follow was *E bello pax*	No instance after 1721	„ II.370	1771
Bring oil to the fire	No instance after Shakespeare, 1605–6	„ V.304	1775
His own mind would be his hell	No instance after Fuller, 1732	„ VII.294	1773
What the people of England never had cannot be lost	One only dated 1653	„ VII.155	1776
The way of all flesh	None after 1631	„ VII.418	1776
Time flies!	None between 1386 and 1807	„ I.197	1776
You are out of her books	None between 1627 and 1861	„ I.166	1771
Riches ... make themselves wings	None between 1607 and 1855	„ VII.473	1785
Art is long; life is short [Latin]	None between 1350 and 1859	„ VII.473	1785
The burnt child dreads the fire	None between 1670 and 1837	„ VII.414	1766
The corruption of the best is always the worst of corruptions	None between 1618 and 1856	„ VII.388	1762
You shall be convinced that there is balm in Gilead	None between 1560 and 1849	„ VII.303	1778
Home is home ... be it ever so homely	None between 1692 and 1826	„ VII.101	1776

The Expression	*O.D.E.P.'s instance(s)*	*Fletcher: Date*	
The golden mean	None between 1642 and 1901	*Works*, V.236	1775
Divide and rule	None between 1633 and 1907	,, V.232	1775
Among friends all things are or should be common	None between 1546 and 1853	,, II.319	1771

In their context it is obvious that Fletcher is not a victim to the lazy recital of trite phrases. His spontaneity will be apparent if his expressions are compared with the definitive proverb forms. His materials are subservient to his spiritual aims; for instance the utilitarian maxim about being on the safe side is used to pave the way for Christian charity, and worldly-wise recognition of the insecurity of wealth is twisted to teach a very other-worldly vigilance.

Literary critics have sometimes spoken as though the language of literature must perforce be different from that of everyday speech. Fletcher did not think so. We can hear the lively language of the market, tavern, racecourse, mine and furnace-house, as well as that of church and chapel echoing through his style. The subject is a study in itself. It can only be touched upon here.

First, then, we point out a few typical expressions, all taken from the *Appeal to Matter of Fact* and its appendix *The Address*:

> The happy medium
> nip in the bud
> in his element
> seal the death-warrant
> hoist the white flag
> go to hell for company
>
> cry down
> infernal crew
> loll out
> parched up
> a cheerful glass

At random we set down a pittance of the great wealth of everyday expressions occurring in other works:

the more the merrier	new-fangled
dead as a corpse	ale-bench
dead and alive	lubberly fellows
sell my last shirt ...	let fly
ready money	chit-chat
mingle-mangle	church-robbers
O Lud [Lord]	

The similarity between Fletcher's style and Wesley's is very marked, especially in the matter of phraseology. Fletcher tells us that he often perused Wesley's *Works*, and it seems most probable that he was influenced by Wesley more than he realized. Nearly all the expressions and single words mentioned in this section on English idiom are found in Wesley. But Fletcher's indebtedness is emphasized by the hundreds of phrasal similarities which lie on the borderland between idiom proper and Revival speech. Here is a sample list of such expressions, frequent both in Wesley and Fletcher:

golden moments	arrows of conviction
tenements of clay (human body)	sins of surprise
	solid happiness, etc.
the mantle of love	Adamic law
saints of the world	the help done on earth
sing a requiem to	throw off the mask
great/thoughtless vulgar	shadow out
dress up as scarecrow	honest heathen
painted fire	relative duties

Wesley was fond of all these expressions: some of them were almost revival jargon. The expression 'relative duties' may well be Wesley's own creation denoting 'Christian duty to one's relatives'.

Fletcher, like Wesley, shows no squeamishness concerning colloquial, rough-sounding, words. If these are, or seem to be 'the Devil's', he will use them to turn the

Devil's arms against himself. The plain word is preferred to a euphemism almost without exception; men, for example, are 'blockheads', 'bedlamites' (fig.), 'brats', 'coxcombs', 'strumpets' or 'tipplers'. They are spoken of as 'broods', 'shufflers', 'flighty', 'dead-drunk', 'bloody', and 'apish'. Fletcher habitually used the adjective 'bloody' with a Jonsonian ring—'bloody bullies', 'bloody adulterers,' 'bloody enthusiasm', 'bloody tyrant', and the like, though not slang, have nevertheless a colloquial sound. 'Animal' figures for human attitudes and emotions are common in Fletcher; sometimes the phraseology is allusive as when he speaks of 'heart-toads' and 'bosom-vipers'. On rare occasions he utters a half-apology for such plain speech.[11]

Now and then he descends (if to use some of the most expressive English is a descent) to outright slang. Thus he speaks of 'seals' meaning 'converts', and 'brass' meaning 'money', whilst 'fleece' and 'stink' used figuratively are near-slang. Colloquialisms such as 'break' meaning 'to fail in business', 'cut' meaning to 'drop' people, and 'puss' for 'cat', are not uncommon.

With the revival of religion came the need for an appropriate terminology, and this jargon (to speak exactly and not offensively) abounds in all the literary works of the movement. Fletcher dropped into it easily—the following are amongst the many which he made to do heavy duty:

bitters (bitter experiences)	never-dying
change (death)	pant
cordials	professor
damps	ranter(ism)
frames	ravish(ings)
free-willers	spirituals
interest	sweets (happy providences)

[11] *Works*, IV.43.

merit-mongers	temporals
moral-men	transports
mourner	wrestling

The hardest worked of them all in Fletcher is the term 'evangelical'—but this represents a distinctive concept of Fletcher's thought which we shall consider in the next chapter.

Before leaving the subject of religious terminology, mention should be made of the many items current which were openly biblical in origin or allusion, items which would have no referent for the majority of today's readers. These, and scores like them, were current-coin:

an acaldema	
babel-builders	Geneva-Diana
a Benjamin's portion	lap of Delilah
blood-besprinkled	painted Jezebel
daub with untempered mortar	stony-ground hearers

(3) *Literary Craftsmanship*

There is a starkness about much of Fletcher's writing which no study of his terminology alone can bring out. We must therefore watch him at work upon sentence, paragraph, and various literary forms.

One who could write of parochial conviviality in the following manner might produce anything: 'You who make it your chief delight to turn your heated mouths into smoking chimneys, your over-loaded stomachs into stewing-pots, and your enormous bellies into moving hogsheads. . . .'[12] It is hard for us to imagine this holiest of men penning such things. There are hundreds of satirical pen-pictures of humanity which have an 'indelicate' ring to the sleek, hypocritical saints of the world. Fletcher could write about circumcising females, and about

[12] *Works*, VII.233.

depriving men of their vitals. He alludes to cutting off the breasts, and of applying aloes to them. He makes the fornicator 'climb up into his father's bed', and he belabours those 'big with bastard child'. His figures are often tortuous, as when he speaks of the 'rape of grace' and of tearing out and reversing a man's tongue. Such muscularity of expression was common in the eighteenth century, as the readers of Swift and Smollet will know. Not that this was any consideration with Fletcher—his authority for strong metaphor lay in Scripture itself.[13]

Scripture, whole chunks of it as well as 'texts', are manipulated by Fletcher with striking freedom and with a degree of novelty. We shall leave on one side normal quotation as a theological authority. Fletcher delighted to use Scripture as soliloquy, monologue, and dialogue. All these can be illustrated by confining our attention to the last-named form. By dialogue we do not mean only formal dialogue—conversation between the lay figures of the writer's creation. This is to be found in Fletcher, with the usual effect when figures are put up for the author (under another figure) to knock down. Dialogue means also conversational style, in which the writer addresses people or gods or devils with the reader listening-in, so to speak. References to particular instances in Fletcher's *Works* will make clear what is meant, and will indicate to the reader the sort of thing to look out for.

In the *Equal Check* a long speech is put into the mouth of 'the judge of all the earth'.[14] Here much of the Scripture language is put into italics. Old and New Testament passages come rolling out, inextricably jumbled up. In addition, the jargon of the Calvinistic Controversy including Fletcher's nonce-items, issue from the deity's lips with the same ease and dignity as Scripture itself.

A little farther on in the same work[15] Fletcher delivers from the lips of Christ a speech nine pages long to one of

[13] Ibid. VII. p. 61.   [14] Ibid. V.72-3.   [15] Ibid. pp. 77-85.

the lay figures named Zelotes. If the reader will examine this utterance he will find that it contains almost every stylistic feature so far mentioned, besides others of a rhetorical nature which we are to deal with shortly.

Antinomian argument, specious and glib, is satirized by Fletcher in many places. If it were not that humour is a desideratum in Fletcher's sanctity, one would say that he almost enjoyed himself in composing these exuberant speeches of ridicule. An excellent example is to be found in the *Second Check*, where a bold Antinomian addresses the Lord in a fine ingenuous mixture of biblical phraseology and biblical allusion.[16]

A much shorter speech, severely ironical in tone and Calvinist in content, is so arranged as to convince the reader of the absurdity and monstrosity of reprobation. Here scriptural language which is attributed to God (Matthew 25) is interwoven with imaginary Calvinistic jargon.[17]

Personal letters, as well as theological works, reveal this feature of scriptural and general dialogue. For instance, in one letter[18] human speech is addressed to God, and the biblical material is allusive, not verbatim. Elsewhere, pastoral encouragement is conveyed rhetorically by means of a divine speech crammed full of scriptural passages distinguished by italics.[19] An instance of Arminian dialogue in reply to Calvinian may be seen in the *Equal Check*.[20]

Another of Fletcher's literary tricks with Scripture is that of putting quaint adjectives with proper names. For instance, in the *Fourth Check* all the following occur:

Obedient Judas	legal Moses
happy Iscariot	Antinomian Jezebel
reprobated Judas	converted Paul

[16] *Works*, II.416-18. [17] Ibid. p. 246. [18] Ibid. VII.360-1.
[19] Ibid. p. 395. [20] Ibid. IV.136-7.

old Solomon	undaunted Caleb
fond Rachel	valiant Joshua

The name 'Adam' takes a good many different adjectives in different Works—these, for example: 'penitent', 'depraved', 'fallen', 'guilty', and 'spared'. Jezebel, in addition to being dubbed 'Antinomian', is elsewhere labelled 'cursed', 'impious', and 'painted'. Paul is 'holy Paul' in one context, 'unconverted Paul' in another. This idiosyncrasy of style runs to surprising lengths with Fletcher—to the point of tiresomeness in fact. If it were rare, things such as 'spared Noah', 'dead Lazarus', 'tempted Job', 'mild Jesus', 'preserved Noah', 'lying Ananias', 'mourning Hezekiah', 'pious Deborah' and 'backsliding Ephraim' would be effective, but the novelty wears off after a time.

Like many eighteenth-century authors, Fletcher does not care to see his nouns standing without their adjectival attendants. When he is not using 'pure' adjectives, he is penning compound nouns which are little different from noun and adjective. Items such as 'forge-hammer', 'half-Christian', 'land-flood', 'thief catcher', and 'letter-learned', 'moon-like', 'self-conceited', have an established dictionary status, but the majority of Fletcher's compounds, whether adjectival or nominal, have a nonce quality about them. Many of them come out of the cut-and-thrust of revival and controversy. An idea of Fletcher's versatility may be gathered from this little representative list:

all-atoning	Necessitarian-Rome
anti-mediatorial	non-necessitating
Christ-debasing	protestant-inquisition
death-exalting	sin-dispelling
death-purgatory	sin-predestinating
double-principled	super-metaphysical
evangelistically-sinless	wide-reprobating

free-returning   will-spring
heart-adultery   wrong-pointed

'Geneva' compounds run into hundreds,—nearly all of them ironical. Even when 'Geneva-logic' is dignified as 'Logica-Genevensis' the irony cannot be hid. Such things as 'Geneva-colossus', 'Geneva-medusa', 'Geneva-purgatory' occur every few pages.

We must now turn away from linguistic aspects of our study to look at Fletcher's craftsmanship with figure, and image, and aphorism.

Theological and philosophical discourse is lit up in Fletcher's style with an abundance of quaint, interesting and sometimes startling illustration. Time and time again he reminds us of Bunyan and Jeremy Taylor. He possessed insight. He saw and felt the supernatural (that means for him the evangelical) in the natural. His biographers recount numerous stories of how birds, beasts, insects, objects and events provided him with opportunities to moralize. This gift he cultivated in literary expression. He believed that 'truth' will merely dazzle (in various degrees) unless it is screened. Thus he speaks of the value of a 'parabolic blind'.[21] His illustrations are of all kinds—patterns, types, allusions, Latin tags, figures of speech, parables, allegories, and such like. We can only hint at Fletcher's wealth in this respect.

Bible names have been mentioned above: these are purposeful and vivid in Fletcher's prose. They incarnate for him the sins, virtues, moods, dispositions, faculties, hopes and fears of humanity. They hold up a mirror to the reader. One of the intensest instances is to be found in the *Second Check*.[22] To people brought up on the Bible a stage-scene involving Cain, Esau, Judas, Dinah, Onan, Absalom, Jonah, Zeruiah and Doeg (to mention only some) must be full of dramatic content. Each

[21] *Works*, IV.176.   [22] Ibid. II.411.

character has his portrayal—in a devastating adjective.

A typical instance of the hundreds of Fletcher's Bunyanesque passages may be seen early on in the *Third Check*.[23] Here he describes a traveller's first sights of a great empire. A man with his arms folded, seated in a chariot, is going off to inherit an estate to which he has no title. Behind the chariot follow five cartloads of broken-limbed prisoners loaded with irons. These prisoners, the traveller learns, were deliberately injured in childhood. They cannot run in the King's race—so they are being carted off, attended by a royal retinue, to punishment and death. Thus the King manifests his absolute power. The parody of Calvinian Theology is all the more forceful because the story or allegory is so vivid. Fletcher believed it impossible to overdraw the picture.

A 'nutshell'-size allegory can be found in the *Equal Check* where Fletcher takes the reader into the making of it. True, i.e. Protestant Christianity is shown as a woman with two lovers who mutilate her in the process of showing their affection. Some of the allusions in this passage are so clever that they can easily be missed.

The illustrative element in Fletcher's style is so massive that some opponents charged him with picture thinking instead of reasoning. He knew how to rebut the charge. 'When the proofs are gone before,' he says, 'just illustrations wonderfully help many readers to detect the fallacy of a plausible argument.'[24]

An aspect of Fletcher's style worthy of study is his ability to make neat, incisive, pithy sentences. Quotable aphoristic phraseology is plentiful. Some have a proverbial ring:

Inconsistency is the badge of error	*Works*,	III.216
Error moves in a circle	,,	IV.22
Error is never more dangerous than when it looks a little like truth	,,	VI.99

[23] Ibid. III.25, 26. [24] Ibid. III.256.

Nature, like Naaman, is full of pre-
  judices   *Works*, VI.388
Fact is fact the world over   ,,   VI.414
It is good to know when to yield   ,,   VII.436

Pastoral advice, likewise, is couched in incisive language:
Let us live to God today and trust him
  for tomorrow   *Works*, I.211
Pray hard, believe harder, love hardest   ,,   VII.421
The followers of Christ are required to
  tread in the footsteps of their Master,
  and not deeply to speculate upon the
  secret things of his Kingdom   ,,   VIII.369

The theology of evangelical Christianity, 'plain food' as Fletcher called it, is set forth in simple dignity, thus:
Judgement certainly finds us where
  death leaves us   *Works*, III.323
As a diamond does not become a pebble
  upon the finger of a papist, so truth
  does not become a lie under his pen   ,,   III.392
Bigots are religious savages   ,,   V.368
Antinomianism which starches, stiffens
  and swells the soul   ,,   VI.330
How easy is it to take the Reformation
  of our manners for the Regeneration
  of our souls   ,,   VII.249
Old light is dead light. A notion of old
  warmth is a very cold notion   ,,   VII.342
Our nature wants to step at once into a
  throne: but he offers first to nail us
  to the tree   ,,   VII.348

Questions of grammar, syntax, spelling and such like fall outside the scope of this study. It must suffice to say that Fletcher's English is on the whole correct. He varies the length of his sentences from the exclamatory term to one of thirty-five lines.[25] But the majority are short, and the reader rarely tires, let alone gets lost. French influence is hardly noticeable. His spelling often seems quaint, but in the eighteenth century spelling was more varied than it is today. Tests made on some fifty Fletcher words have revealed that his variations, in nearly every case, are recorded by the *O.E.D.* as being customary at that time. The great exception is the word 'woe' which he always spelt 'wo'—a form obsolete since the thirteenth century.

(4) Religious Spirit—Rhetorical Dress
'Rhetorical propriety is not theological exactness', Fletcher once wrote,[26] but he did not conclude that theology has no need of rhetoric. Doubtless he was inconsistent: he scorns 'oratory', yet by all accounts he was a master of persuasive speech. He discountenances rhetoric, yet he shows passion and skill in persuasive writing. What is that but rhetoric? We have Wesley's testimony that Fletcher preached with all his might, and there are many who witness that his written works influenced people's beliefs and conduct.

In a way, Fletcher preaches in all his writings. Much of what has already been said in this chapter bears on the question of rhetoric. It remains to emphasize certain aspects of style which are, as it were, tricks of the trade of persuasion. First then, Fletcher had been trained in rhetoric and he appeals to it on occasion.[27] Again, he remembers that the Bible is crammed with rhetorical figure, and he appeals to this fact in connection particularly with catachresis and hypotyposis—two figures eminently associated with liveliness of style.[28] Rhetorical figure occurs in everything except the actual balancing of texts in the *Scripture Scales*. His adjectives are emphatic,

[25] *Works*, VI.29-30. [26] Ibid. VI.207.
[27] E.g. ibid. p. 198. [28] Ibid. III.173, VI.198.

and when they are massed it is not for academic purposes. For example, when he writes that men 'must remain unrestored or they must have an almighty, omniscient, omnipresent, unwearied, infinitely patient Saviour', that is emotive, not simply theological. There is emphasis and vitality (two fundamental principles of rhetoric) in such constructions as this: 'Ye taste those powers, happy believers, who see that God is love, boundless, free, redeeming, pardoning, comforting, sanctifying love.'[29]

Among the devices which have given rhetoric a bad name is that of 'apostrophe' which we may call a playing to the gallery in print. There is much of this in Fletcher. He cries out 'Hail Wesley! Hail Henry!' [Matthew].[30] 'Hail Adam under the fatal tree.'[31] He apostrophizes the Early Church thus: 'O ye Halcyon days!'[32] He makes cracks in the earth speak with the voice of the Deity, crying: 'O Earth, Earth, Earth!'[33] He addresses Paul in the middle of an argument.[34] Often Fletcher writes at white heat. He warns and he woos, he soothes and he satirizes, he reasons and he rebukes. He has you in a corner one moment with his 'Thou art the man': he lets you loose upon eternity the next moment and shows you the Millennium. Exclamation marks may be a literary weakness—but Fletcher scatters them by the hundred.

On the other hand, Fletcher is an inveterate satirist. His irony is as obvious as his intensity. He spotlights mental, moral and spiritual 'trimming', all shuffling and hypocrisy. He recommends only *mild* irony, recognizing its dangers, and counselling that no one should dip his pen in irony until he has soaked it first in the oil of divine love.[35] He sought to use it as a surgeon uses a lancet.[36] Similarly with logic. Truth is to be pursued that way, but love is to be used in the detection of error.[37] He was

[29] *Works*, IV.230. [30] Ibid. II.256. [31] Ibid. III.87.
[32] Ibid. II.339. [33] Ibid. VII.246. [34] Ibid. II.261.
[35] Ibid. III.246. [36] Ibid. p. 463. [37] Ibid. V.368.

acknowledged as one of the mildest and most modest controversialists in literary history.

Fletcher endeavoured to be plain enough for mechanics yet not beneath the dignity of clerics.[38] It was perhaps hoping for too much. Educated people would be stretched by his vocabulary; much of it was inappropriate to common people. Doubtless clerics formed his main public, but lay people of the wealthier classes read divinity in his day. Lay leaders of Methodism certainly studied his works.

His prose, perspicuous, interesting and lively, is, at its best, as good as anything that came out of the Evangelical Revival. It must be judged against that background. But even at this distance of time it still speaks to the discerning reader.

---

[38] Ibid. IV.280.

CHAPTER FOUR

Christian Thinker

FLETCHER's saintliness has impressed nearly all writers on English Religion in the eighteenth century. His abilities as writer, preacher, and evangelist have also been pointed out. But it seems that no one has thought it worth while seriously to study his thought. Obviously nothing on a full scale can be attempted in a single chapter of a volume covering several aspects of his ministry; what is here aimed at is a conspectus of his teaching. The chapter is headed 'Christian Thinker' because we are not thinking of him simply as a theologian, nor simply of the end-product of his teaching, but we shall be concerned with his reasoning processes as well.

Leighton Pullan in his *Religion since the Reformation* gives a niche to Fletcher, who was, he asserts, 'a theologian of no mean ability'. All the same, it was not Fletcher's intention to write as a systematic theologian. The theological content of his *Works*, no less than their literary form, was governed largely by his apologetic purpose. Controversy, not contemplation, made him a writer, and frequently it was scurrility and not scholarship that he had to counter. However, his thought is crystal-clear, and his spirit scholarly and restrained.

1. TEMPER OF THOUGHT

Only one who was himself proficient at prayer could safely say of the popular George Whitefield at the height of a revival of heart-religion that he was better at praying than at thinking. The observation is made in a passage which is an allegory of Fletcher's own method in controversy—'. . . the truly Reverend Mr Whitefield understood far better how to offer up a warm prayer, and preach a pathetic sermon than how to follow Error into her lurking holes in order to seize there the twisting viper with the tongs of Truth, and bring her out to public view, stript of her shining dress, and darting in vain her forked, and hissing tongue'.[1] To show up error and to reduce it to absurdity and so to impotency is plainly in the forefront of Fletcher's mind. He is Truth's terrier, holding on and shaking his quarry until there is no more spirit in him.

For instance, Richard Hill, author of *Pietas Oxoniensis*, probably with no intention of mitigating David's sin with Bathsheba, speaks a good word for him thus—'David was still a son, though a perverse one'. Fletcher fastened like a leech on that and never let go all through his *Checks*. To the point of tiresomeness he reiterates his favourite ironical opposition to what he considered Hill's leniency, in the phrase, 'David in Uriah's bed'.[2] This is Fletcher's big stick with which to beat anything that even looks in the direction of antinomianism. This is the *reductio ad absurdum* of any faith or reasoning which Fletcher thinks is morally weak at the centre.

Fletcher is rarely content with the minimum in argument: he lays on his strokes until he himself tires. For example, in rebutting the pseudo-scriptural argument that good works are dung, dross, and filthy rags, he takes twenty-one biblical passages which contain the phrase 'good work(s)', and writes them out substituting the former terms for the scriptural. Reason does not require such repetition, and indeed Fletcher half apologizes for, as he puts it, taking up the 'filthy rags of this bad divinity though it is only with the point of the pen'.[3]

In the controversial warfare Fletcher is extremely

[1] *Works*, V.171. [2] E.g. ibid. III.187; V.95.
[3] Ibid. III.222-3.

assiduous. He fights to win on every line; he fights in depth on all fronts. No matter what the issue, he always seems to have a massed contingent at his command. Notably, this is true of his employment of Scripture. Although he is not a proof-text thinker, yet he does mass biblical texts and passages in a way which makes some readers want to skip whole pages. A good instance of his method occurs in the *Last Check*. After he has assembled many of St Paul's expressions in the first person to prove that Paul's religious consciousness supports the Methodist doctrine of Perfection, he is still unsatisfied. He continues: 'This description of the perfect Christian . . . appears to me such a refutation of the Calvinian mistake which I oppose, that I cannot deny myself the pleasure, and my readers the edification, of seeing the misrepresented apostle give his own lovely picture a few more finishing strokes.'[4] Fletcher is here unwittingly portraying himself. He is ever determined to be in at the kill.

This spirit produces faults of literary style, but it does not necessarily lead to injudiciousness of thought. Fletcher's ideal of Christian ministry included judiciousness. He had unbounded admiration for Wesley—not only on account of his apostolic labours, but for those mental qualities which, Fletcher claimed, made Wesley the John Goodwin of the age.[5] Wesley was, in Fletcher's view, 'a judicious divine'.[6] Judiciousness of thought and perception was an ideal after which Fletcher strove, and it is to the judicious reader that he addressed his arguments and made his appeals.

As this concept, more than any other, explains the temper of Fletcher's thought, it will be well to make clear what is meant by it. The concept is a rich one. In general it means an awareness of all the factors in a situation and the ability to weigh them and judge them. In particular it means the ability to reason in matters of religion with

[4] *Works*, VI.219.   [5] Ibid. II.262.   [6] Ibid. VI.356.

mental, moral and spiritual integrity. Its antithesis in the Fletcher vocabulary is the term 'dotages',—a term which he frequently employed to connote religious discourse springing from weak-headedness. But 'judiciousness' is not simply an intellectual attribute, it includes the notion of wisdom—the ability to draw the right practical as well as the right intellectual conclusions. Hence, in one place Fletcher writes of the 'judicious mariner' as one who can read his chart and steer his ship by it. On this analogy he believes that he is himself a 'judicious protestant', that is, one who could interpret the gospel map which 'exhibits the boundaries of truth, the crooked shores of the sea of error, the haven of peace, and the rocks rendered famous by the doctrinal wrecks of myriads of unwary evangelists'.[7]

This passage makes clear that a 'judicious divine' must essentially be an 'orthodox' divine; he could not so reason as to support say Pelagianism, or Antinomianism, or Calvinism. When Fletcher speaks of 'judicious Calvinists'[8] it is clear that their judiciousness lay in their recognition of valid Arminian claims.

'Balance' is the outstanding characteristic of Fletcher's thought. He maintains that the whole Truth must be, and can be retained in an organic unity. Fletcher has thus a three-fold mental ministry: first, he must avoid the extremes of opposing doctrines; secondly, he must achieve positive balance of antithetical truths; and thirdly, he must reconcile not these truths only, but those who hold them, in a charity greater than intellectual agreement or disagreement. The most fitting emblematic representation of Fletcher would, therefore, be one which shows him kneeling upon a full orb, holding the scales between his suppliant hands.

Fletcher, then, seeks the *via media*. For instance, with regard to the fundamental theological question of Faith

[7] Ibid. V.213.   [8] E.g. ibid. IV.11, V.76.

and Works, he quotes a passage from Bishop Beveridge (interlarding it with his own parentheses—a favourite trick) and adds 'the saving truth lies exactly between the mistake of Zelotes and the error of Honestus'.[9] Arminius is congratulated by Fletcher upon the way he steered between the Pelagian shelves and the Augustinian rocks.[10] But it is to Cranmer that Fletcher turns to find the very incarnation of the *via media* principle. 'To the honour of this favoured isle', he writes, 'and of perfect protestantism in a happy moment he [Cranmer] found the exact balance of the gospel axioms.'[11]

The reader can find Fletcher's own summary of the *via media* in the closing pages of the *Equal Check*—'Let every evangelical doctrine have its proper place in our creed, that it may have its due effect upon our conduct. Consideration, repentance, faith, hope, love and obedience have each a place on the scale of gospel truth. . . . Whilst the philosopher exalts consideration alone; the Carthusian, repentance; the Solifidian, faith; the Mystic, love; and the Moralist, obedience; thou Man of God, embrace them all in their order, nor exalt one to the prejudice of the rest.'[12] Fletcher then proceeds in his own quaint, fascinating way to warn against cock'd-hatted religion, frumpish religion, partisan religion, bigoted religion, and love-less religion.

It is not enough merely to avoid extremes. Fletcher believed that Truth, Christian Truth, is symmetrical. He argues this out at length with supporting quotations from Scripture and from Patristic and Reformation authors. But what catches the imagination are the many figurative enforcements of his arguments. In the *Equal Check* alone the notion of the wholeness and symmetry of Truth is illustrated by reference to classical mythology, biblical anecdote, to landscape gardening, human anatomy

[9] *Works*, V.52. [10] Ibid. p. 248.
[11] Ibid. p. 235. [12] Ibid. p. 364.

(truth is double-breasted, etc.), marriage, architecture, politics, measurement, motion, warfare, ship-building, and optics—to name only some.

Fletcher's dominant concern as a Christian Controversialist was to reconcile men, not simply notions. He made a plea for a 'Society of Reconcilers' and enforced it by pathetic reference to worldly-wise unity. The 'unhappy divisions'[13] amongst Christians (how up-to-date it sounds) wrung from him the satirical parody of one of Charles Wesley's noblest verses:

> *Love has not our pride destroy'd*
> *Render'd our distinctions void:*
> *Names, and sects, and parties rise:*
> *Peace retires and mounts the skies.*[14]

The concept of 'judiciousness' therefore, as it concerns a divine, includes mildness, courtesy, and Christian charity. Fletcher does not use Wesley's phrase 'catholic love', but he exemplified it to a notable degree. This must be kept in mind or our remark about his being in at the (doctrinal) kill will be misleading. Truth is not merely mental. He conceded that it is better to be doctrinally wrong with his antagonist, Dr Crisp, than practically deluded with those whose profession was orthodox but whose morals were suspect.[15] The acid test of doctrine lies, for Fletcher, in its fruit of character.

Before leaving the subject of Fletcher's thought in general, several further observations may be set down. We have referred to his clarity of thought. This needs to be extended so as to include the note of certainty. The Christian in the modern world, adrift in an ocean of queries and conjectures, is challenged by the assurance of Fletcher's thinking. Like Wesley, he airs no doubts. Like Wesley also, he was skilled in logic. But the clarity and certainty we have mentioned is rather that of

[13] *Works*, II.315. [14] Ibid. V.384. [15] Ibid. III.106.

perception than of mechanics, although it authenticates itself in the sphere of mental mechanics. First, there is in Fletcher an enviable sureness of touch with terminology. He knew the hazards of loose definition. His thinking is characterized by nicety of distinction which many of his contemporaries and many writers since, never attained to. An excellent example is to be found in his *Answer to Toplady's Vindication of the Decrees*. To that writer's ambiguous uses of the terms 'must' and 'necessity', Fletcher opposes a series of distinctions which play havoc with Toplady's reasoning. 'Necessity', says Fletcher, 'may be that of duty, of civility, of circumstances, of convenience, of decency, of prudence.' Toplady is welcome to the lot, says Fletcher, but he cannot get Calvinian Necessity out of any or all of them.[16] Doubtless, Fletcher's analytic ability annoyed his opponents. It embarrassed his friends, at times, as when he distinguished four justifications.[17] But anyone who will take the trouble to read the passage referred to will admit that he has the last laugh over the Calvinistic comics who tried to make him look foolish.

Again, Fletcher is adept at getting to the heart of a question, and expert at summarizing. The following passage, for instance, is a theological cameo of the vast subject of the relationship between Divine Providence and human sin: 'It is concerned about it four ways. First, in morally hindering the *internal* commission of it before it is committed. Secondly, in *providentially* hindering [at times] the *external* commission of it when it has been intentionally committed. Thirdly, in marking, bounding and over-ruling it while it is committed. And, fourthly, in bringing about means of properly pardoning or exemplarily punishing it, after it has been committed.'[18] Fletcher's *Works* contain many such neat passages.

Linking with these two features is a third which may be

[16] *Works*, VI.67.   [17] Ibid. III.253ff.   [18] Ibid. VI.104.

called 'nimble-mindedness'. Fletcher is intensely alert. This quality had been noticed by Wesley, who likened it to 'light cavalry' as contrasted with his own 'heavy foot'. Fletcher lights up the dull theological warfare with flashes of brilliance, with irony, with wit, with dexterous touch. Almost any page would afford instances, but we will select the formal, polite conclusions of the letters which make up the *Checks*. These are witty summaries of all that has gone before, the last nail, as it were, in the controversial coffin: e.g. 'Yours in the bond of a peaceful gospel'. '. . . a free and peaceful gospel', '. . . a practical gospel', '. . . St James's gospel', 'Yours in the Liturgy, Articles and Homilies of the Church of England', and so on.

II. PROTESTANT PAR EXCELLENCE

Fletcher's admiration of the Protestant Fathers and his detestation of Roman errors have already been mentioned. Later in this chapter when we deal with his teaching on his doctrines of grace, we shall consider special aspects of his protestantism. In this section we shall examine Fletcher's account of the Protestant position and measure him against it.

His birth and training, particularly his University training at Geneva, had given him an advantage over all his English Calvinistic opponents. He had first-hand knowledge of the literature of the Continental Reformation. He was well-versed also in the history of the Movement. This is clear from identifiable quotation, and also from allusion. A large amount of his phraseology is derived from the great protestant writers of the Continent. But these writers do not hold him in thrall; his appraisal of them is well-balanced, and he does not hesitate to point out their shortcomings. He writes: 'When the first Reformers shook off the yoke of papistical trumperies, that fought gallantly for many glorious truths. But it is to be wished that whilst they warmly contended for the simple, scriptural dress of the primitive gospel, they had not forgotten to fight for some of its very vitals. . . . Luther, the German Reformer, being a monk of the Order of Augustine was so busy in opposing the Pope of Rome, his indulgences, Latin masses, and other monastic fooleries, that he did not find time to oppose the Augustinian fooleries of Fatalism, Manichaean necessity, lawless grace and free-wrath.'[19] A similar independent judgement is passed upon other Reformers such as Bucer, Calvin, Erasmus and Peter Martyr.

The student of the Reformation in England is struck by the fact that Cranmer loomed so large in Fletcher's eyes that he hardly noticed any other English Father. There are glancing references to such men as Nowell and Laud, but the present writer cannot recollect any reference to Hooker—'the Judicious Hooker'. Fletcher seems to take English Protestantism as a ready-made thing, and his own views apparently needed no support from English authors, outside the Liturgy, Canons and Articles.

As we should expect, Fletcher's own protestantism is clear-cut and well-balanced. A protestant, he says, is one who examines any system of truth in the light of reason, scripture and conscience. This trio he calls 'the three most formidable batteries in the world'.[20] This is elsewhere clarified with respect to the Reformers thus: 'The Reformers . . . protested three things in general: (1) That right reason has an important place in matters of faith; (2) That all matters of faith may and must be decided by Scripture understood reasonably, and consistently with the context, and (3) That Antiquity and Fathers, Traditions and Councils, Canons and the Church lose their authority when they depart from sober reason and plain scripture. These three general protests are the very ground of our religion when it is contra-distinguished from Popery.'[21]

[19] *Works*, V.234-5. [20] Ibid. III.367. [21] Ibid. IV.276.

SAINT 75

Fletcher was himself governed by the Canons of Protestantism which he promulgated. For instance, he believed that he had reconciled St Paul with St James, and both with reason, conscience and the oracles of God.[22] Moreover, he insisted that Protestantism itself is to be judged by the same three-fold test. Whatever is unscriptural, irrational, immoral, no matter if it has the semblance of an angel of light, is to be exploded as 'big with the most impious consequences'.[23] Indeed the test is fundamental all through the processes of arriving at Truth, and applies to reason, scripture and conscience themselves. Although Protestantism comes to define itself against the Papal System, it is, in fact, a Method—perhaps we might go so far as to call it the ultimate criterion of Christian being, and the way thereto.

Having named the Protestant Trinity, we must now examine their relationship in Fletcher's thought.

(1) *Reason*
In almost every case Reason is first-named. Fletcher seems absolutely untroubled by problems of epistemology: man is treated as though he is innately 'reasonable'. This does not mean that he views reason humanistically. Nothing human is unaffected by the divine Spirit. Man is never without divine grace—which he has according to the 'dispensation' he lives under. Of course, Fletcher holds that only 'right reason'[24] is valid, i.e. reason which is self-authenticating and consistent with revelation. Reason is for Fletcher fundamental: without it experience is meaningless, and revelation impossible and conscience uneducable.

In spite of the passionate and the rhetorical, to which we referred in the previous chapter, there is a prevailing tone of reason in all Fletcher's writings. Often it might be Aquinas or Hooker speaking. In a passage, for instance,

[22] Ibid. III.329. [23] Ibid. V.442. [24] E.g. Ibid. V.127.

contrasting the faith of a fanatic with that of a 'rational Bible-christian'[25] he writes: 'The one extinguishes the torch of reason that he may have opportunity to display in its room the vain flashes of his own pretended inspirations: the other entertains a just respect of reason following it as the surest guide, so far as it is able to direct him in the search for truth; and whenever he implores a superior light, it is merely to supply the defects of reason. The one destroys the clear sense of scripture language that a way may be made for his own particular manifestations: the other refers everything to the Law and to the Testimony, fully satisfied that if high pretenders to sanctity speak not according to this word it is because there is no light in them. The former flatters himself that while the means are neglected the end may be obtained, presuming that God will illuminate him in a miraculous manner, without the help of prayer, study, meditation, sermons or sacraments: the latter unpresumingly[26] expects the succours of grace in a constant use of the appointed means; and conscious that the Holy Scriptures are able to make him wise unto salvation he takes them for the subjects of his frequent meditation, the ground of his prayers, and the grand rule of his conduct.'[27]

Many of Fletcher's most clearly-reasoned passages relate to the 'Horrible Decree' of Reprobation or to lawlessness in religion. Such passages seem tedious today, for the love of God is taken for granted and religion is assumed to be 'doing good'. Perhaps Fletcher's most pungent use of reason is in those passages where, by the use of logic, he shows up the absurdities of Calvinian and Antinomian thinking.[28] He suits his form to the general reading public, e.g. he frequently uses the enthymeme,

[25] For the phrase, cf. *Works*, IV.279.
[26] Unpresumingly—N.B. a form and usage unrecorded in the *O.E.D.*
[27] *Works*, VIII.301-2.   [28] E.g. ibid. VI.99, 245-6.

but he maintains that the formal logician will not be able to fault his logic on this account. He maintains, too, that behind popular illustrative form there lies sound reasoning.[29]

(2) *Scripture*

For Fletcher the Scripture is a 'Creation' in which man has to dig and explore. Like creation, it is assumed to possess pre-established order and harmony. Like creation (as viewed in Fletcher's day) it possessed solidarity, even 'finality'. Hence the assiduous industry and the mental energy expended by divines to 'get at' its treasures. Hence also the schemes, the types, the analogies, which the literary critic dismisses with contempt.

Fletcher is restrained in this use of Scripture, but he reveals incredible industry in associating passages and in setting passages in apposition on a linguistic basis. If he kept the context in mind—and often he seems not to have done so—he paid no regard to date. He could identify Old Testament theophanies with Christ;[30] he could speak of the King of Israel as Christ in His pre-existent nature.[31] All Scripture has to be reconciled, and it is all reconcilable. There is hardly a hint of doubt in Fletcher's mind about his method; the nearest approach to it is in connection with Samuel's words, which Fletcher quoted. He reflects that Samuel might be considered unevangelical, and so he seconds his point with a New Testament quotation.[32] All Scripture is authentic, equally authentic, it would seem. This is the framework within which traditionalist scholarship had to work. Thus, in comparing Peter and Jude, to take but one instance, it does not occur to Fletcher even as a possibility that both are not equally authentic.[33]

It would be quite mistaken, all the same, to think of

[29] Ibid. II.25.   [30] Cf. ibid. VII, 350ff.   [31] Ibid. IX.229.
[32] Ibid. V.34.   [33] Ibid. V.42-3.

Fletcher as an untrained biblicist. Within the traditional framework, which is an intolerable strait-jacket to a modern critic, Fletcher shows striking freedom. To attempt to interpret Scripture 'reasonably' is to be, so far, a critic. To balance Scripture, as he does in the *Scripture Scales*, is critical in a quaint fashion, for the work contains a good deal of Fletcher as well as Scripture.

On the numerous occasions where he mentions textual and exegetical points, Fletcher reveals his competence in biblical scholarship of the standard of Bengelius.[34] On other occasions, as when he appeals to the minutiae of the Apocalypse to settle a question of human righteousness, he is the relentless controversialist rather than the biblical scholar.[35]

Another characteristic feature of Fletcher's use of Scripture is to interlard his quotations with running commentary and interpretation. So prevalent is this habit that we are apt to conclude that he rarely lets the Scripture speak for itself. Sometimes the comment or interpretation is doctrinal and absolutely ties down the meaning for controversial purposes, as is the case with the text 'The soul that sinneth [personally] it shall die [eternally]; every one shall die for his own [avoidable] iniquity.'[36] In other cases, Fletcher's interlardings are literary or exegetical, as in this instance: 'There is no speech or language [no country or kingdom] where their voice is not heard. Their [instructing] line went through the earth [their vast parish] and their words to the ends of the world [their immense diocese]. For the invisible things of God [that is, his greatness and wisdom, his goodness and mercy], his eternal power and godhead, are clearly seen, being understood by the things that are made [and preserved] so that they [the very heathen who do not obey their striking speech] are without excuse....'[37]

[34] E.g. *Works*, VI.71. [35] Ibid. III.304-5.
[36] Ibid. III.24. [37] Ibid. III.12-13.

On occasion Fletcher's brackets are so frequent and so long that a mental effort is needed to see him through.[38]

(3) *Conscience*

In his emphasis upon conscience Fletcher takes his stand beside Luther, as regards individual freedom, although he warns against unnecessary singularity. He was, as has often been pointed out, the champion of moral fruitfulness against pharisaism (by which he very often means Romanism), enthusiasm, ranterism and antinomianism. But, in a way which is rarely noticed, he was 'modern' in his application of the moral test to those doctrines which are not usually considered experiential, for example, the doctrine of God. The *Equal Check* contains a very penetrating passage in which the Calvinist doctrine of Absolute Predestination is viewed in the light of the moral being of God as Predestinator. A God who could so act, Fletcher maintains, cannot be the God and Father of Christ and men; he must be bad, unjust, unveracious, unholy, unwise, inefficient, unsovereign—and much more. The whole passage is worth reading.[39]

It may seem, at first sight, that Fletcher's Protestant batteries leave no room for any appeal to Christian tradition. It is true that he utterly repudiates tradition in the Roman sense as an authority alongside of Scripture. Further, he appears to take little or no cognizance of Church History, except the pre-Nicene and the Reformation periods. But as a priest of the Church of England he knew that an age-long tradition was not discarded at the Reformation but re-shaped nearer to the apostolic model. He used a Liturgy in lineal Catholic descent. He refused Presbyterian ordination when abroad. He stood upon the historic creeds as symbols of Catholic faith.[40] But this brings us to a fresh division of our subject.

[38] E.g. ibid. IV.444-5.   [39] Ibid. V.172-4.
[40] Ibid. VIII.287-8.

III. CHAMPION OF ORTHODOXY

Fletcher is Protestant. Fletcher is also Catholic—not in the sense of unessential points of ritual, but in the massive sense of patristic theology. He concludes the first part of the *Equal Check* on this truly 'catholic' note: 'All creeds therefore, like that of St Athanasius, and all faith must end in practice. This is a grand article of what might, with peculiar propriety, be called *the catholic faith*—the faith that is common to and essential under *all* the dispensations of the everlasting gospel in all countries and ages, "the faith, which except a man believe *faithfully*", i.e. so as to work righteousness like the good and *faithful* servant "he cannot be saved".'[41] That is Vincent de Lerins himself, with a distinctive Fletcher emphasis.

Doctrine is for Fletcher the source of right conduct. In the places where he is most Protestant, naming the two grand Reformation doctrines, he also issues a warning against over-emphasis.[42] Protestantism, to be sane, needs the full Trinitarian Faith. The catholic doctrine of the Trinity was not abandoned by the reformers, Fletcher teaches, and when it is fully grasped it preserves all that is essential to Christianity. What Fletcher wrote against Priestley is directed also against Voltaire, Hobbes, Spinoza, Rousseau, Montesquieu, Hume and company: it is not a change of controversial front, but a defence of the doctrinal centre of Christianity. His *Rational Vindication of the Catholic Faith* is a most able piece of work.

We, today, who glibly acknowledge the Trinity, would profit by the Methodist apprehension of its reality. To Wesley, as to Fletcher, it was not a theory, but a triple mode of redemptive activity. Heresies such as Arianism and Socinianism are ever present, and are not notions of the head only. They are a denial of the Godhead and

[41] *Works*, IV.110. Fletcher's italics.
[42] Ibid. IV.25 (a good instance of his allegorical style).

are thus hindrances to full salvation. Fletcher will not contend, any more than Wesley, for the term 'Trinity', as it is not in the Bible, but plainly the thing is there.[43] No Christian doctrine is safe, Fletcher holds, if full Trinitarianism is rejected. If Christ be anything less than Deity, and if the Holy Spirit be not Christ carrying on His own redemptive work in Sanctification, then mankind is unredeemed and without hope. To Fletcher, the doctrine of the Trinity is 'the capital doctrine of Christianity'.[44] Fletcher's catholicism is nowhere more clearly seen than when he teaches that except on the basis of Trinitarianism, as fact, our Baptismal Covenant is meaningless, and no spiritual religion can spring from it. If God be not Father, Son and Holy Spirit, man is without a Saviour and a Sanctifier.[45]

Doctrinal emphasis and exactitude are associated in some minds with aridity in religion itself. Fletcher is the very man to refute this. We will not enter into the mystical field, in which Wesley also showed interest, of the possibility of an experimental knowledge of the Trinity. We here draw attention simply to the richness of Fletcher's thought and experience of God as manifested in the variety of the language used of God. He needs a hundred epithets in constant use. The list following gives some of the favourite expressions:

Ancient of Days	Lord of Lords
Artist, Original, etc.	Majesty of Heaven
Author	Ocean of Excellence
Benefactor, the Heavenly, etc.	Omnipotent Creator, Proprietor, etc.
Examinator	Original of Virtue, etc.
Father of Lights, Mercies, etc.	Parent of Good
	Physician of Souls

[43] Ibid. II.281. [44] Ibid. IX.29. [45] Ibid. IX.26-7.

Fountain of Perfection, etc.
Gracious Rewarder
Heavenly Physician
Infinite Wisdom, Goodness, etc.
Judge of Earth
Keeper of Israel
Kind Protector
King of Saints, etc.
Lawgiver, Eternal, Great, etc.
Preserver of Men
Protector, Almighty,
Punisher, the Just, etc.
Searcher of Hearts
Sun of Beauty
Supreme Being, Majesty, etc.
Transcendent Effulgence
Trier of Reins

Most of these derive, of course, from Scripture, but they do more than reveal an intimacy with the Word of God; from a sincere pen they indicate intimacy with God himself.

John Fletcher is the antidote to those who ground evangelism in anything less than catholic doctrine. He is also a standing rebuke to those who think that doctrine unfits a man for effective evangelism.

IV. EVANGELICAL PROPHET

The hardest-worked term in the Fletcher vocabulary is the word 'evangelical'. We shall try to give shape to Fletcher's conception later on. In the meantime let it be said that it is in no sense a party label. When we call him Evangelical Prophet we mean that he burns to rescue men not simply from erroneous doctrine, but to lead them into happy and holy fellowship with God and men. In theological language we mean that he emphasizes the 'doctrines of grace'.

We have previously mentioned Fletcher's 'misanthropical' references to children. Theologically, these run back to his beliefs about the Fall of Man. It is axiomatic in his thinking that humanity is corrupt. It is axiomatic also that man will not, or cannot, forsake sin even when convicted of it. He writes: 'Never did a besieged town dispute the ground with such obstinacy, and hold it out by such a variety of stratagems, as those whereby corrupt man stands out against the repeated attacks of truth and grace. . . . He feeds on the dust of the earth; he tries to fill his soul with the husks of vanity; and fares hard on sounds, names, forms, opinions, withered experience, dry notions of faith, empty professions of hope and fawning shows of love, till the famine arises, and the intolerable want of substantial bread forces him to surrender at discretion and without reserve.'[46]

Human sinfulness is, then, the starting-point of Fletcher's evangelical thought. The place of this in Christian doctrine is unequivocably stated thus: 'Take away then the doctrine of the Fall, and the tower of evangelical Truth built by Jesus Christ is no more founded upon a rock, but upon the sand; or rather the stately fabric is instantly thrown down and leaves no ruin behind it, but the dry morality of Epictetus, covered with the rubbish of the wildest metaphors, and buried in the most impertinent ceremonies.'[47]

The work from which this passage is taken, i.e. *The Appeal to Matter of Fact and Common Sense*, piles up the evidence of man's corrupt state. It is a heart-rending account of human misery, of disordered nature punishing disordered people in a disordered society. Fletcher appears determined to say all that can be said and so finds the proof of his argument in natural philosophy, classical writers, human history, parish wakes, and in other spheres. The superior modern cannot restrain his smile upon reading that agriculture, road-making, commerce, government, education, linguistics, indeed civilization itself are contingent upon the Fall. It is so easy to forget that as recently as Fletcher's day, most of these were

[46] *Works*, II.100.   [47] Ibid. II.139.

supported by no other power than the aching human body. But even in a sweat-of-the-brow order of things there were objections to Fletcher's views. 'Man's pleasures counterbalance his calamities', it was urged, to which he retorts that sickness, say toothache or gout, 'damps every worldly joy, while all earthly delights together cannot give us ease under it'.[48]

There is a starkness about Fletcher's thought which a sentimental age finds revolting. Fletcher's case is overdone, maybe, but it is essentially, even crushingly sane. The sentimentalist forgets the sinfulness of sin in fitful human goodness. Fletcher confronts him with his ruthless logic. To the objection that 'calamities prove a blessing to some' he replies: 'And so does transportation: but whoever inferred from hence that reformed felons were transported for the *trial* of their virtue and not for the *punishment* of their crimes?'[49] It is sin, insists Fletcher, that man needs to be saved from. He hardly ever, in all his writings, talks of being saved from 'Hell'. When he does mention Hell it is in ways strikingly similar to modern psychological conceptions. We see here the sanity of his insistence: if man is saved from sin to evangelical (this includes moral) righteousness, he must be saved from Hell —however it is thought of.

Man is fallen. Yet man is free and responsible. No one fought more tenaciously than Fletcher did to preserve this dignity to men. Necessity, whether philosophical or theological, had in him an implacable foe. Just as he defends the Faith at its doctrinal centre, so he exposes the central weakness of Calvinism, Materialism, Deism, i.e. at their denial of man's moral freedom. 'The moment the doctrine of Necessity is overthrown', he writes, 'Manicheism, Spinozism, Hobbism, and the spreading religion of Mr Voltaire, are left without foundation, as well as that part of Calvin's system that we object against.'[50] Once

[48] *Works*, II.46.   [49] Ibid. II.47.   [50] Ibid. V.457.

surrender freedom and responsibility, he proceeds, and it will be hard not to confuse matter and spirit.

In evangelical doctrine man's freedom is thought of as exercised in 'Faith'. Fletcher thinks of faith much more realistically, more psychologically, than Wesley does. He does not speak of it, as Wesley did, as a supernatural ἐλέγχος. He hesitates even over the phrase 'saving faith' lest it be thought of as some gift or endowment from God to some favoured individuals. Theological faith, he says, is 'believing heartily'. It is not essentially different from any other kind of faith. It is a subjective-objective or divine-human relationship, an activity not essentially different from eating, moving and breathing. As the object of appetite is food, so the object of faith is God. Faith is the human being—heart, mind and will—apprehending God, receiving God, and responding to God. On this view Fletcher has no Faith-Works problem, for as a man cannot breathe in without breathing out, and as the heart cannot have systole without diastole, so faith is that grace which is receivable from the divine Spirit only to be uttered back to God in real-life motion of love and works.[51]

Faith, then, is response. But to what? To the love which God has for man. Fletcher commends the Roman emphasis of the Atonement, although he does not argue the doctrine and seems untroubled by theories about it. Perhaps this was because Rome, Geneva and Anglicana were in closer agreement at this point than at some others. Better than theories is this delightful little passage, which, although it is about human sanctity, tells us how the divine love treats man: 'He who walks in the light of the divine love sees something of God's spiritual, moral or natural image in all men, the worst not excepted; and at the sight that which is merely creaturely in him (by a kind of spiritual instinct found in all who are born of the spirit) directly bows to that which is of God in another.'[52]

[51] *Works*, IV.10-11, 156-7, 200, etc.   [52] Ibid. II.367.

When Fletcher realized and cast himself upon the love of God he became a new man, and he never tired of proclaiming the evangel.

The doctrines of grace, specifically Justification, Regeneration and Sanctification, all receive what we may call 'Reformation' emphasis in Fletcher. The last of these we shall leave on one side here, as it is essentially the object of spiritual direction which occupies us in the next chapter. Regeneration also need not detain us long, as Fletcher is thoroughly 'Evangelical' in insisting that all goodness is of the divine Spirit, and that Grace alone can renovate human nature. But there is a balance in Fletcher in the matter of Regeneration which is absent from many protestant thinkers.

Most noticeably, and like Wesley himself, he rarely spoke of 'Conversion'. He speaks much of the Holy Spirit's work within us yet not so as to detract from Christ's work for us. Both Puritan and Quaker extremes are avoided in his insistence upon vital union between what Christ did and what he now does in his Spirit.[53] Fletcher speaks far more of the Baptismal Covenant than he does of Conversion. There is but one hint in all his *Works* which may be construed as a doubt about Baptismal Regeneration and even this is not certain.[54] There is no doubt that he held firmly to an objective spiritual activity coincident with, if not absolutely tied to Baptism.

Turning to the doctrine of Justification we become aware of unusual complexities in Fletcher. He asserts the primary Reformation doctrine of 'Justification by grace through faith'.[55] Man, to be in a harmonious relationship with God, has to trust Christ—this harmony cannot be 'merited' by man. But Fletcher seems to think of Justification as continuous, rather a state than an act at the beginning of a state. He speaks of a second justification, and indeed of several justifications.[56] It seems that his

[53] *Works*, III.112. [54] Ibid. I.69. [55] Ibid. II.25. [56] Ibid. III.46.

passion for balance is responsible for this line of thought. Fear of Quaker and Antinomian excesses, the one on the practical side and the other on the nominal, leads him to attempt to preserve in balance the truth which each contends for. The stress on 'works', whether by Quaker or Papist, has to be toned down by emphasis upon 'Faith'. And the stress on human meritlessness—on Faith as the medium of forgiveness—has to be toned up by emphasis upon action, or 'works'. So, the first justification reinstates us in 'the *favour* of God; the second reinstates us in the *image* of God'.[57]

Fletcher defends his notion of justification at length. It cannot be falsified, but it is a needless complication of theological science. His second justification often appears to be a post-mortal declaration of holiness; if so it is included in the doctrine of sanctification.

What Fletcher attempted, and what he thought he had achieved is best given in his own words: 'The doctrines of grace which we maintain do equal justice to the divine attributes:—defend faith without wounding obedience;—oppose pharisaism without recommending antinomianism;—assert the truth of God's promises without representing His most awful threatenings as words without meaning;—reconcile the Scriptures without wounding conscience and reason;—exalt the gracious wonders of the day of atonement without setting aside the righteous terrors of the great day of retribution;—extol our heavenly Priest without pouring contempt upon our divine Prophet; and celebrate the honours of His cross without turning his sceptre of righteousness into a Solifidian reed, His royal crown into a crown of thorns, and His *law of liberty* into a *rule of life* by which His subjects can no more stand or fall in judgement than an Englishman can stand or fall by the *rules of civility* followed at the French court.'[58]

As a theological aim, that would satisfy a papal college

[57] Ibid. II.340.   [58] Ibid. III.459-60.

of doctrine. As a protestant manifesto it condemns much that goes by the name of Evangelicalism as thin, spineless, lifeless. The Evangelical, as Fletcher taught it, is massive, well moulded and virile. It would need a volume in itself to do Fletcher's Evangelicalism justice. It can be summarized thus: The Evangelical is not necessarily identical with Protestantism, Methodism or Sectarianism. Neither is it necessarily anti-Catholic, anti-Roman, anti-Quaker. If it is anti anything it is anti-sin—but then, all Christian thought is that. In defining itself, of course, it necessarily condemns what it holds to be erroneous. But it is not Fletcher's part, nor is it the part of Evangelical Christianity to snipe in a rear-guard action. By an Evangelical Christian he means one that is Christian after the Bible pattern, the real thing all-alive and no sham, one in whom the moral and spiritual image of Christ is to be seen, and to be seen ever more clearly.

This view is supported by his use of the term 'evangelical' in its adjectival and adverbial forms. The adjective alone qualifies over three hundred different nouns, some of which occur scores of times. It is used along with biblical proper nouns, as when he speaks of 'evangelical Paul'. It can denote a type of preaching and a type of congregation. When used along with abstract nouns such as 'Truths', 'Axioms' or 'Principles' it denotes the distinctively Christian fundamentals, often carrying a hint of their having been forgotten or overlooked by the Church in history. Another application of the term is to history as the sphere of Revelation and Redemptive Activity thus—'evangelical epochs', 'evangelical dispensations'. Again, it can mean the 'Revelational' as distinct from the moral or philosophical. Or it can mean the 'Divine', as when he speaks of 'evangelical charity' as being the image of God. Once again, the term often seems to denote the experiential as against the formal, as when he speaks of 'evangelical sorrow', 'prayer', 'penitence', 'obedience', and so on.

SAINT

But the evangelical itself may be counterfeit, and Fletcher is obliged to speak at times of the 'scripturally evangelical'. On other occasions the term is practically equivalent to 'Arminian', as in phrases such as 'evangelically worthy', and 'evangelically legal'. But occasionally as in the phrase 'evangelical penance', it suggests the Protestant as contrasted with the Roman. Finally, there is in Fletcher an extensive figurative usage, as when he speaks of the 'evangelical crown', 'ironies', 'millstones' and 'trumpets'.

V. CHRISTIAN PHILOSOPHER

We turn now to consider several aspects of Fletcher's thought which lie in the borderland between theology and philosophy.

When his *Works* are read together and with attention, it will be manifest that he has a distinctive favourite doctrine to which he gives the name 'The Dispensations'. In the Preface to the Second Part of the *Equal Check* he avows this doctrine thus: 'As I make my appeal to true Protestants, I lay particular stress upon the Scriptures. And there I find a doctrine, which for a long succession of ages has been partly buried in the rubbish of Popery and Calvinism. I mean the doctrine of the various dispensations of divine grace towards the children of men; or the various talents of saving grace, which the Father of Lights gives to Heathens, Jews and Christians.... I make a constant use of this important doctrine. It is this chiefly which distinguishes this tract from most polemical writers upon the same subject. It is my key and my sword. With it I open the mysteries of election and reprobation; and with it I attempt to cut the Gordian (should I not say, the Calvinian and Pelagian) knot.'[59]

If in that context the doctrine of 'dispensations' seems narrowly controversial (although both Calvinism and

[59] *Works*, IV.283-4.

Pelagianism imply wide questions of philosophy), elsewhere it is so wide as to amount to a philosophy of history, and even a metaphysic.

Fletcher holds that there is one purpose which binds all creation and thus all human history into a unity. On the divine side it is Revelational; on the human side it is Redemptive. Everything is to be referred to 'the manifold wisdom and variegated goodness of God'.[60] All God's works are perfect in their place and the gradations of perfection express his will and reason.[61] Fletcher's thought is thus 'world accepting', and like the great Catholic thinkers, he links 'nature' and 'grace' in an ascending scale.[62]

In history, therefore, God makes providential use of whatever furthers his will. This is the meaning of historical election and reprobation—Fletcher uses these terms, drawing their Calvinistic sting to show that they mean choice or rejection according to God's good purposes.

It is not only in Sacred History, that the process operates, although it is seen most clearly there. Without using the term 'Progressive Revelation', Fletcher makes much of the concept. He did not work it out critically regarding the Scripture itself, but in applying it to non-biblical, non-christian history, he shows himself more enlightened than many of his contemporaries. All history has value, though not all equal value. Whereas many Christian thinkers either refused to face the issue concerning the heathen, or relegated them to a gloomy prospect, Fletcher, by his 'Dispensation' doctrine, granted them a purposeful history and hopeful future.

Concerning biblical and Christian history, manifesting clearly God's increasing purpose, Fletcher sees analogies in physics, biology and everyday life. Those 'who call nothing gospel but the last dispensation of it should

[60] *Works*, V.306. [61] Ibid. VI.179. [62] Ibid. VI.180.

remember that as a little seed sown in the spring is one with the large plant into which it expands in summer; so the gospel in its least appearance is one with the gospel grown up to full maturity'.[63]

Fletcher's largeness of view made nonsense of Calvinian narrowness. It reveals a Deity infinitely rich in being, purpose, grace and power. Fletcher finds a place for everything in the divine order of dispensations, which he enumerates in one place as 'coelestial, paradisaical, royal, gentile and Christian'.[64]

Fletcher's enemies mocked his doctrine as 'romantic flights of the pen'.[65] He thought it simple, reasonable, moral, and Christian. He writes: 'Let nobody say that the doctrine of these degrees of acceptance is founded upon metaphysical distinctions and exceeds the capacity of simple Christians; for a child of ten years old understands that he may be accepted to run a race before he is accepted to receive a prize; and that a man may be accepted as a day labourer and not as a servant; be as a steward and not as a child; as a friend and not as a spouse. All these degrees of acceptance are very distinct, and the confusion of them evidently belongs to the Calvinian babel.'[66]

Although he was too busy to study non-christian religions seriously, yet Fletcher moved along the road towards the evaluation of religions as manifestations of one fundamental human activity. He was almost twentieth-century in maintaining that Christianity stands by no other test than that of value. Some may think he spoilt his achievements by writing 'Calvinism is Christianity obscured by mists of pharisaic election and reprobation, and by a cloud of stoical Fatalism. Popery is Christianity under a cloud of pharisaic bigotry and under thick fogs of heathenish superstition.'[67] We must remember, however, that he

[63] Ibid. III.10; cf. IV.330. [64] Ibid. III.336. [65] Ibid. V.339.
[66] Ibid. III.47. [67] Ibid. III.449.

was not writing as a university professor, but as a pamphleteer.

We leave the 'Dispensations' to consider his view of miracle. Here, also, Fletcher has an enlightened judgement. He practically ignores the traditional view that proved the divinity of Christ by his miracles. At times, it almost seems that the gospel miracles were an embarrassment; not that he disbelieved them, but that they have little value for faith now, as indeed was the case when they were performed.[68] The great miracle, to Fletcher, is that Christ can manifest Himself today so as to convince believers of His presence. The spiritual miracle of opening the eyes of human understanding is for him greater than the restoration of physical sight.[69] Fletcher's work entitled *The Spiritual Manifestation of the Son of God* is worth reading if for no other reason than because it anticipates insights with which we have become familiar—as the psychology of religious experience. There is almost a twentieth-century ring about his view that Christianity must validate itself. The final miracle, to which no external test can be applied, is that God permits man the vision of himself, and offers him fellowship with himself.

Of Fletcher's politics there need be made only the briefest mention. His views were exactly those of Wesley. Indeed if Fletcher's *Vindication* and his *American Patriotism* are compared with Wesley's *Calm Address to our American Colonies* it might well be concluded that they came from the same pen. Fletcher is a High-Church Tory in politics, but this does not preclude an appeal to the Articles of Calvin on the subjects of civil government, and civil obedience.[70] Tyerman records that King George desired that Fletcher should be rewarded for his services to the country in writing the political tracts. But the Government was powerless to reward a man who desired only more of the grace of Christ.

[68] *Works*, VII.363. [69] Cf. ibid. IX.365. [70] Ibid. VII.50.

VI. MILD ESCHATOLOGIST

A certain mildness and reticence characterizes Fletcher's thought about the 'Last Things'. The spirit fits in well with his own large charity, and is especially consonant with his 'Dispensations' doctrine. Threats of Hell and of everlasting punishment, and the appeal to fear are almost non-existent in his writings, although sometimes in preaching and in conversation, he warned the obstinate sinner that he must 'either turn or burn'. The dispensations which follow death are linked rationally, spiritually, purposefully with those of life. The post-historical dispensations similarly are linked with the historical. Each change of growth is 'perfect in its kind', and the final changes, whenever they take place, must be the best of all.[71] In this sense, Fletcher acknowledges himself a 'perfectionist'. It by no means follows that all men must be saved in the end, but it follows that if men respond to the light they have they will be promoted in growth towards perfection.

Tyerman, on the strength of a single passage, categorically asserts that Fletcher was a 'Millenarian'. Presumably he means that Fletcher believed in an imminent 'Return' of Christ to the earth coincidental with a partial resurrection in order to the setting up of an apocalyptic Kingdom —the reign of Christ and the Saints for a Millennium— which will end with the final Resurrection and Consummation of all things. True, in this one place[72] Fletcher does speak of a dispensation which has not yet occurred and which is to take place before the Second Coming of Christ. But as he speaks of this as historical, and almost identifies it with the post-pentecostal period, it is doubtful whether Tyerman has grounds enough for his claim. Fletcher's conception of progressive dispensations could be used as grounds for the counter claim. The truth is

[71] Ibid. VI.178ff.   [72] Ibid. V.217-18.

that Fletcher's thought is rich and scintillating, and he cannot be neatly classified and labelled. Certainly his mentality was not millenarian in the sense of indifference to social and ecclesiastical progress, although he shared the deep seriousness of those who held millenarian views.

His views of death, although those of a Christian realist, were mild, and warm, and human. When his friends die in the faith he does not think of them as derelict, or in a state of half-life, or as being denuded. So his friend Perronet is spoken of to Miss Perronet as 'My now ever-living friend'.[73] To a father whose child has died Fletcher writes that 'one more cherub has been added to the heavenly host'.[74] He encourages a mother to look forward to her own death where she will 'soon have the joy to meet her [daughter] as an incarnate angel'.[75]

Perhaps in the intensity of apocalyptic vision he foreshortened the future. Certainly with the detachment of the mystic he annihilated time. Certainly, too, in the faith and fellowship of Christ, death surrendered to him its sting and opened the gate to the richest dispensation of all. 'Christ is the blest point of unity,' he writes, 'a point this which fills heaven and earth—which runs through time and eternity.'[76]

---

[73] *Works*, VII.449.   [74] Ibid. p. 448.
[75] Ibid. p. 425.   [76] Ibid. p. 449.

CHAPTER FIVE

Spiritual Director

IN FLETCHER'S presence men became aware of God and of the spiritual realm to an extraordinary degree. Men of the highest probity, some of them by no means novices in the spiritual life, witness to this fact. If the testimony were rare it would be dismissed as exaggeration, but it is common and has to be accepted. Moreover, the impression was constant throughout all the ups and downs of Fletcher's life, public and private, in sickness and in health, languishing or recovering.

The biographers make good use of the testimonies to the aura of sanctity which surrounded his person. Here we shall confine ourselves to two such. The first is the awed whisper of one who visited him at death's door—'I went to see a man that had one foot in the grave. I saw a man that had one foot in heaven.'[1] The second is the record of a Methodist preacher who spent a few minutes with Fletcher in a stableyard in Bristol—'Dismounting from his horse he [Fletcher] came towards us with arms spread open, and his eyes lifted to heaven. His apostolic appearance, with the whole deportment, amazingly affected us.' When, a few minutes later, Fletcher took the travelling preacher's refreshment, and in the yard blessed it and shared it out in sacramental fashion, the little company was overwhelmed. Said James Rogers: 'Such a sacrament I never had before. A sense of the Divine Presence rested upon us all; and we were all melted into a flood of tears.'[2]

[1] *Works*, I.216.   [2] Ibid. I.235.

I. THE MYSTERY OF GODLINESS

Such influence may be inexplicable. Holiness is a mystery which does not yield its secret to probing or analysis. The saint himself is usually quite unable and would probably be unwilling even if he were able, to explain what he radiates. He is exceedingly willing to share it, but he cannot do so as it is a supernatural work. For at the centre of holiness is a paradox of unawareness and unselfconsciousness, so that the greater the saint the stronger his disclaimer to sanctity. At the same time, in the nature of the case, only the saint knows the inner side of sanctity. Only one who is treading the spiritual way realizes its reality, and knows its laws, its hazards, and its impediments.

Fletcher would probably have been unhappy at the mere thought of himself as an exponent of the spiritual life. There is no evidence that mystical or ascetic theology were ever his special studies. He had no opportunity, in a remote English village where religion was almost dead, of being a Curé d'Ars. Amongst his writings there is no treatise like De Sales's *Devout Life* or Scupoli's *Spiritual Combat*. Apart from his Genevan origin, there was little in eighteenth-century Anglicanism to call for such things: the English Church generally has been negligent in the study of the principles and practice of the spiritual life.

All these facts render Fletcher's Writings the more significant for our study of his spiritual teaching. A systematic work on Christian piety, from his pen, would be a treasure indeed. But it would not be more compelling than the Holy Wisdom which is scattered throughout his writings. Here he gives us many insights of his own spirituality, and many glimpses of the laws which govern it. In his *Works* there is a wealth of spiritual teaching with none of the drawbacks of over-systematization. They are not 'reflections' upon the spiritual life—such easily become a post-mortem—they are his own life and thought meeting real life, and recording real life.

It will be necessary, of course, to extract this teaching, and put it into some sort of order. But we shall be wary of getting everything methodized but mystery-less, lined up but lifeless, scientific but soul-less. All the same, we may indicate Fletcher's essential 'soundness' in this realm by saying that time and time again as he speaks, we might be listening to any of the great Catholic Masters. Indeed, he avows that the language of the saints is one the world over. As he puts it: 'Christ the way is everywhere, and faith in His word is, like His word, one and the same in every age and country. So is holiness, the narrow way.'[3]

II. THE AIM OF THE SPIRITUAL LIFE: UNION WITH GOD BY MEANS OF CHARITY

The grand aim of religion, Fletcher teaches, is union of the soul with God. Perhaps his clearest statement of the aim occurs in the *Appeal to Matter of Fact and Common Sense*— 'The spiritual life of the soul consists in its union with God, as the natural life of the body does in its union with the soul: and as poison and the sword kill the latter, so unbelief and sin destroy the former.'[4]

Everything that Christianity permits or prohibits is governed by this grand aim. Everything has value or lacks it in relation to this aim. For instance, in a passage full of common sense and yet rich in spiritual wisdom, Fletcher deals with the differing degrees of Godly sorrow, which different men experience. He insists that it is the end that matters, and that end is the same for all, namely, 'to come to Christ to be made partakers of His merits, holiness and felicity'. He continues: 'The sorrow which

[3] *Works*, VII.455.   [4] Ibid. II.121.

answers these ends is quite sufficient, though it should be ever so light, and of ever so short a duration. On the contrary, a distress as heavy as that of Judas is unavailing, if instead of driving us from sin to Jesus Christ, it only drives us from profane-ness to hypocrisy, or from presumption to despair.'[5]

Union with God is, then, the object of Christian spirituality. If it were always remembered that God is love, nothing need be added. But because union with God is sometimes conceived in terms of pantheism or mysticism, which might or might not produce 'character', but which would certainly stop short of love in the gospel sense, it has been the practice of the great Christian Masters to include in their definition of the grand aim a statement of the grand means, i.e.—'by means of charity'. Paradoxically, charity the means is also of the nature of an end in itself. In scores of passages Fletcher sets forth the full aim of the spiritual life as that of union with God by means of charity. He never tires of insisting that charity or love is the image of God, the way to God, fellowship with God, and the manifestation of God. The *Portrait of St Paul* is a sustained commentary upon the text 'now abideth faith, hope and charity, but the greatest of these is charity'. He joyfully quotes Augustine on this issue as being in harmony with St Paul—'You then speak from the Spirit of God when you speak from a heart glowing with love'.[6] Elsewhere we find Fletcher setting forth the supremacy of charity, with characteristic illustrations. 'Faith is the hidden root, hope the rising stalk, and love, together with good works [this tautology is for Antinomian consumption] the nourishing corn: and as the King's agents who fill a royal granary do not take the roots and stalks, but the pure wheat alone; so Christ takes neither faith nor hope into heaven, the former being gloriously absorbed in sight, and the latter in enjoyment.'[7] Not many lines

[5] *Works*, II. p. 170.   [6] Ibid. VIII.305.   [7] Ibid. II.332.

SAINT

farther on he asserts that 'love is both the nature and the element of the saints in glory'.

Nor does Fletcher leave his readers in any doubt as to what the charity is by means of which men are in union with God. He writes—'Charity consists of two parts, patience and benevolence. By the one we suffer every kind of indignity without entertaining a thought of revenge; and by the other, we heap upon our enemies unsolicited favours. Our adorable Master, whose conduct has furnished us with examples of the most perfect charity, discovers to us the extent of this virtue in the following passages. . . . [Here follow quotations of our Lord's words.] From these expressions it appears that our Lord would have His disciples to possess a charity not only extraordinary in some degree, but altogether divine. In point of quality, He requires that it should be equal to the inexpressible love of the Father; as a drop taken from the ocean is of the same nature with those mighty waves that roll over the unfathomable deep.'[8]

III. SCOPE OF THE SPIRITUAL LIFE

(1) *The Nature of Perfection*

The grand aim of religion is not a distant goal which has religion as a temporary expedient. Union with God is a present experience in so far as charity reigns in the heart. But sin, and the conditions of our mortality, are obstacles to our fellowship with God. We shall deal with Fletcher's practical directions on these issues later; here we must notice that the grand aim of spirituality has to be worked out in the human situation of moral evil and physical mutability. In relation to these the Aim is defined as 'Perfection'.

Fletcher deals with this thorny subject at length in the *Polemical Essay* which forms the second part of the *Last Check* published in 1771. After deep, sustained thought

[8] Ibid. VIII.255.

and prayer he came to what he admitted were 'alarming conclusions'. First, that 'there is no medium between pleading for the continuance of indwelling sin, and pleading for the continuance of heart-antinomianism'. Secondly, that 'All who attack the doctrine of an *evangelically sinless* perfection deserve, *when they do it* (which I hope is not often) the name of *advocates for sin* better than the name of *Gospel Ministers* and *Preachers of Righteousness*'.[9]

Without wading into this controversial issue we may say that Fletcher was so afraid of complaisancy and delusion—of anything less than completest perfection of which the soul is capable, that he went to the other extreme. In spite of Fletcher, a spiritual director can say that sin remains in the Christian without pleading for its retention. Such could, in fact, fight sin to his dying day. Hill was right in reminding Fletcher of Articles IX and XV which state that the infection of sin and actual offence remain in believers. The root of Fletcher's over-emphasis was his abhorrence of the Roman post-mortal purgatory and of Calvinist death-purgatory. Christ alone frees the soul from sin, and this Fletcher's doctrine of 'Evangelical Perfection' asserts.

Clearly the Christian Perfection which Fletcher taught, and that which he experienced himself allows of growth. Whether it be called sin, or whether it be called by a relative term, such as imperfection, the saints lament their unworthiness. Fletcher constantly deplored his lack of love, humility, and so on. The Perfection he held, and this point needs emphasis, is the 'perfection of sincerity'. We are perfect under God's disposition of all the circumstances of our life, when all within us tends towards God. We find this same doctrine clearly expressed in the *Fifth Check*, where Fletcher maintains that the only perfection men are capable of is that of fallen creatures in process of renewal. The perfection of Paradise cannot be

[9] Fletcher's italics.

ours. Fletcher writes—'Innocent men with unimpaired powers could yield perfect obedience to the law of innocence; therefore that law made no allowance, no provision for any deficiency in duty. Not so the law of liberty, for, although it allows no wilful sin, yet it does not reject sprinkled, though as yet imperfect obedience. Nor does it, as some divines would persuade the world, curse the bud because it is not yet the blossom, or the blossom because it is not yet the fruit, or the fruit because it is not yet ripe; provided it tends to maturity and harbours not insincerity, the worm that destroys evangelical obedience'.[10] The remainder of the passage is a most hopeful assessment of human status and talent. It asserts that God expects of us only what we have it in our power to give.

On the manward side the spiritual life is response to God—to God known, loved, and to be obeyed. Hence perfection is a matter of the whole man, that is, as Fletcher many times says, of the understanding, the will and the affections. This is not a theory. Fletcher worked out his own salvation in these realms, and sought to claim these powers in others for Christ. He wrote to the 'serious' people at Madeley urging them, and pledging himself to stand to the baptismal vow, and to follow the law of love, in the words: 'I am not at all discouraged, but determine with new courage and delight to love my neighbour as myself; and to love our *Covenant God*, Father, Son and Holy Ghost, with all my mind, heart and strength; with all the powers of my understanding, will and affections. This resolution is bold, but it is *evangelical*; being equally founded on the precept and promise of our Lord Jesus Christ, whose cleansing blood can atone for all our past unfaithfulness, and whose almighty spirit can enable us to perform all gospel obedience for the time to come.'[11]

[10] *Works*, III.397. [11] Ibid. I.223 (Fletcher's italics).

(2) *The Place of the Understanding*

God cannot be loved unless he is known. So we arrive once again at the point where Doctrine is realized to be a necessity, or at least where Truth must be realized as such, and to be comprehensible, and to be dependable. Hence, Fletcher is constantly speaking of 'saving truths'. The 'catholic faith' is the parent of catholic piety, and the wholeness of the parent is reflected in the balance of the child. Truth of course, for Fletcher, is not 'notions' far less speculation: it is that which is deemed to be final for human calculation—all calculation, whether of the understanding, the will, or the affections. As Fletcher puts it: 'Truth is the heavenly seed that produces living faith; and living faith is the heavenly root that produces good works. Truth and faith, therefore, are at the bottom of every good work. . . . On the other hand a lie is the hellish seed that produces unbelief.' Men are converted or perverted, Fletcher says, by their principle of action, by their 'predominant practical belief.'[12] The saints are those who, in the language of scripture 'have truth in their inward parts', or in less formal language, who stake all on the Gospel's being true.

The importance of Reason in Fletcher's theology has been emphasized in Chapter 4. He constantly sets forth its importance in the spiritual life also. He believed he had St Paul's authority for this, in that Truth is first-named in the apostle's list of Christian pursuits. He writes: 'As soon as obedient *faith* allows *Truth* to sit upon the throne there is an end of mental anarchy: all things resume their proper ranks and places. Creatures in great degree disappear before their Creator; earth before heaven; and time before eternity. Thus Satan's charm is broken, God begins to be to us, what He is in Himself, *all in all*; and when we *see* Him such, if our faith be lively and practical,

[12] *Works*, IV.191.

we *treat* Him as such: we answer the end of our creation; Truth prevails; Satan falls as lightning from Heaven; man is man, and God is God.'[13] That might be Thomas Aquinas himself.

It does not follow that a man must be a theologian to be a saint. What Fletcher means is that sanctity is not safe, and perhaps, in the full Christian sense, not possible, except on the basis of truth. As we shall see later on, speculation and 'evil reasoning' threaten the spiritual life.

Fletcher allows that a man may be mistaken in points of doctrine and yet be truly pious. There are holy souls, he agrees, who are unaware of the issues and importance of the controversy between Calvinist and Arminian theologians. But it is not therefore to be inferred that piety is independent of truth: just the contrary. It is the extremes of both schools which Fletcher regards as unimportant. He clearly states that it is not upon their peculiarities, but upon their orthodoxy that both Calvinian and Arminian piety rests.[14]

Sometimes Fletcher gives Truth a place equal to Charity, as when he insists 'that it is not possible for Christian piety to exist without the brilliant light of truth and the burning zeal of charity'.[15] But the apprehension of truth by the understanding is, after all, a means to the end of union with God. We know in order that we may love, even though there may come a point where knowledge and love, light and warmth, coalesce, and where we know only when we love. This is the point, probably, where we may speak of the intellectual love of God—but Fletcher would probably have disliked that phrase. He put it this way: 'The field of Truth is as boundless as the divine perfections. . . . These three capital truths only, God is—God is love—God is mine in Christ, are more than sufficient to replace my soul in paradise.'[16] Fletcher

[13] Ibid. IV.196. [14] Ibid. V.354.
[15] Ibid. VIII.21. [16] Ibid. IV.180.

rejoices in the prospect of eternity in which to explore truth, but the fact remains that the little he knows here, is the essential stepping-stone to fuller knowledge ahead.

This is reason enough for facing death with the utmost realism. At that crisis above all others the soul needs Truth. 'Were I to come to that awful moment', he writes, 'I would beg of God to keep me from all delusions, and to strengthen my heart-felt faith in Christ, that I might be clothed like a wise virgin with a robe washed and made white in the blood of the lamb, that is, with the righteousness of a living faith working by love; for such a faith is the blessed reality, that stands at an equal distance from the antinomian and pharisaic delusion.'[17]

Closely linked with knowledge of God is knowledge of self. The importance of this branch of Christian Understanding is frequently emphasized by Fletcher. Many times he quotes Solon's maxim, 'Know thyself'.[18] Often, too, he cites the ancients[19]—Plato, Horace, Seneca—as agreeing with Scripture in asserting that the knowledge of sin is the first step towards salvation from it. True knowledge of God, Fletcher teaches, will lead to true knowledge of humanity.

(3) *Control of the Will*

'The unregenerate will is pregnant with inconstancy,' says Fletcher.[20] With the honesty of the keenest satirists he shows up human weaknesses in this connection. In the midst of revival it was absolutely necessary although it was not less courageous on that account, to keep a firm hold upon the fact that piety is precarious unless it possesses itself of the will. No Catholic Director was more certain of this than Fletcher was. We have seen that he personally endeavoured to love God with the understanding, with the will and with the affections. He urged all, rich and

[17] *Works*, III.310. [18] E.g. ibid. VIII.14.
[19] E.g. ibid. II.102, 152. [20] Ibid. p. 62.

poor, high and low, to do likewise. In a lovely spiritual letter to Lady Mary Fitzgerald he writes: 'You still complain of vile self: I wish you joy, for your knowing your enemy. Let vile self be reduced to order, and though he be a bad master, he will become an excellent servant. If you say, How shall I do this? I reply, by letting the Lord, the Maker, the Preserver, the lover of your soul, ascend upon the throne of your thoughts, will and affections.'[21]

The centrality of the will in this trinity is not simply a matter of accident or assonance. That order is reasonable —and in fact Fletcher hardly ever varies it. In an allegorical passage he speaks of the soul as a chariot drawn by the steeds of faith and love. He does not actually say that the will is the charioteer, but he does say that 'the steeds mutually draw the steady chariot of [the Christian's] profession across the valleys of discouragement, and over the hills of difficulty which he meets with in his way to heaven'.[22] Plainly, it is the will that keeps the chariot heading heavenwards. Incidentally, in this allegory, Fletcher sees the steed of faith dropped at heaven's gate, whilst the steed of love draws right in to heaven itself. The precedence of the understanding in the spiritual life is that of time not of order; as we have said, we cannot love God until we have some conception of his nature and person.

Elsewhere in Fletcher he states unequivocally that the will is the faculty above all others that piety must shape and direct. 'All sorts of truths,' he writes, 'if they are kept in their proper places, may improve the understanding; but religious truths only have a direct tendency to improve the will, which is the spring of our tempers and actions.'[23]

As far as Fletcher goes he is absolutely sound. Perhaps the subject of human will appeared simpler to him than it does to us. He admitted that it could not be forced—

[21] Ibid. VII.465.   [22] Ibid. II.216.   [23] Ibid. IV.175.

that it has to be persuaded. He does not tell us how this is to be done, nor has he any method of strengthening the will beyond prayer and making inward acts of desire and purpose, and the refusal to be daunted. He does hold that the soul has the power to attend to truth. He exhorts to patience, and endurance. As a spiritual director he stirs up his people to 'wrestle' with God and with the world, the flesh, and the devil. The soul can if it will 'break through' in spite of 'damps', indolence, heaviness and temptations. Fletcher relies upon the divine Spirit to lead men into the light as they can bear it, and to give men strength to persevere.

The 'Perseverance of the Saints'—a phrase which was sometimes construed on a 'once a saint always a saint' basis—means for Fletcher that where the intention is right, where there is sincere desire to know, love, and obey God, that soul will not be lost. Provided the soul is doing what it can, God takes the will for the deed. Fletcher put it neatly in the language of spiritual science thus to Joseph Brown—'Simplicity of intention and purity of affection will go through the world, through hell itself'.[24]

The doctrine of 'intention' is important in Fletcher's spiritual teaching. Intention is a work of the will. Here lies the root problem for the human soul—how so to want to know and love God as to be dissatisfied with anything less. The soul must 'abide steadily purposed', and Fletcher believes it can be done. To a woman of frail and ailing physique he cried: 'Get willing, truly willing under the Cross and keep there to keep your will in continual subjection to the will of God.' This same woman raised with Fletcher a query concerning 'luminous joy'—almost revival jargon for a sort of mystical experience—to which he replied 'God's design in withholding . . . those gracious influences which work upon and melt the sensitive, affectionate part in the soul, is to put us more

[24] *Works*, I.182.

SAINT 107

upon using the nobler powers, the understanding and the will'.[25]

(4) *The Affective Element in Piety*
Those who think of Methodism as primarily personal, or 'experimental' religion as it was called in the eighteenth century, may be surprised at Fletcher's remark that the understanding and the will are 'nobler powers'. The hymn line which runs 'My God! I know, I feel Thee mine' is frequently an expression of fervency rather than of knowledge. God cannot be 'felt' truthfully, until he is known; it is true, of course, in its turn, that God 'felt' means that he is better known.

Fletcher by no means under-rates the affective or emotive elements in Christian spirituality. He personally was not afraid of them—indeed it seems certain that nothing less than deepest and purest emotion in himself can account for the tears, the sighs, the 'melting' experiences which people felt in his presence. (Melting is another of the hard-worked revival terms.) Provided the emotional is anchored in and tested by the enlightened understanding and the obedient will, it is contributory to 'full salvation'. There is a wealth of emotive language in Fletcher's writings. Religious experience that constantly calls into play such terms as 'adorable', 'amiable', 'cordial(s)', 'mourning', 'pathetic', 'ravish', and 'ravishing' (subst.), 'relish', 'shake' and 'transports', to mention but a few, must be far removed from even the warmest philosophical interpretation of life. In Fletcher's case, however, it must be remembered that vast quantities of the technical language of theology are also found; it is the conjunction of this and the emotive which is remarkable.

What has Fletcher to say on the subject of the affections? First, in general. One of the commonest expressions of the Evangelical Revival was 'frames and feelings'.

[25] Ibid. VII.404.

Those who emphasized personal religion tended to see in 'frames and feelings' the authentic marks of vitality in religion. Those who hated 'enthusiasm', especially those who never learned to distinguish the genuinely Christian emotion from the spurious, turned the expression 'frames and feelings' into one of disparagement. Fletcher is balanced here, as nearly everywhere. Whilst exalting the understanding and the will he maintains that the affections must function in religion. 'None but a dead man', he writes, 'is destitute of "frames and feelings".'[26] He cannot think of light without heat. If the context of this quotation is examined, Fletcher's sanity of judgement will be seen at once. For he allows no emotion but that which stands the moral test; by their fruits ye shall know them. Some 'frame and feeling' must consist with faith and works. If it be of extraordinary intensity it should be received thankfully, as of God, but such 'feelings' are not to be sought, neither are they to be made the criterion.

Fletcher taught that evangelical religion purified and rectified human affection, and he showed up man's lamentable need of redemption and stability in this sphere. He writes: 'Good God! What are his *affections?* Almost perpetually deficient, or excessive. When do they attain to, or stop at, the line of moderation? Who can tell how oft he has been the sport of their irregularity and violence? One hour we are hurried into rashness by their impetuosity: the next we are bound in sloth by their inactivity. Sometimes every blast of foolish hope, or ill-grounded fear; every gale of base desire or unreasonable aversion; every wave of idolatrous love or sinful hatred; every surge of misplaced admiration or groundless horror; every billow of noisy joy or undue sorrow, tosses, raises, or sinks our soul; as a ship in a storm which has neither rudder nor ballast. At other times we are totally becalmed; all our sails are furled, not one breath of devout

[26] *Works*, IV.187.

or human affection stirs our stoical, frozen breasts; and we remain stupidly insensible, till the spark of temptation, dropping upon the combustible matter in our hearts, blows up again into loud passion; and then, how dreadful and ridiculous together is the new explosion!'[27] The man who knew the human heart to that extent neither scorned, nor feared, nor doted upon the feelings. The scope for grace in the affections is obviously wide and deep.

More particularly we notice what Fletcher has to say about the love of Jesus, i.e. sometimes our love for Him, and at others, His love for us. To a lady who looked to him for spiritual direction, he wrote, concerning faith in Christ: 'That this faith may be firmer on our part let it be *rational* as well as affectionate; *affectionate* as well as rational.'[28] Leaving on one side what he says concerning the rational, he continues thus: 'Shall we not believe *affectionately* also? Let us stir up ourselves to love this Jesus, who hath given Himself to us with all His blood, all His grace, and all His mercy. Come, give Him your whole soul, my dear friend, and take Him with all His pardons, all His love, all His strength. If He wants you to embrace Him in His faint, bloody sweat, or on His racking tortures on the Cross, draw not back; love Him, love Him, and let not the grave frighten you: it is good to drop our clay in His quiet sepulchre, and to follow Him on the wings of faith and love without a clog of sickly flesh to heaven.'[29] The devotional manuals of Roman Catholicism could hardly exceed that.

When the love of Jesus possesses the soul all selfish and unstable emotion must yield. As Fletcher puts it to Lady Mary Fitzgerald: 'When Christ is formed in the soul we are so taken up with the wonder of His love, and with praising our Father's mercy and the Saviour's love and tenderness, that there will be little time left to speak

[27] Ibid. II.64-5.   [28] Fletcher's italics.   [29] *Works*, VII.419.

either of good or bad self.'[30] Fletcher believed in the expulsive power and the soul-freeing power of its highest possible affection—the love of God. All the branches of affective piety spring from and are related to this love, for instance, sorrow for sin and the joy of the Lord take their colour and strength from the grand passion of Christ's love felt and returned. Incidentally, Fletcher is no advocate of a religion of misery. Like Charles Wesley he encouraged the dancing heart and spoke of bursts of triumphant mirth, and peals of ravishing praise.[31]

The calculations of the head, and those of the heart, are sometimes, Fletcher acknowledged, hard to reconcile. Although 'Truth' is basic for him, it was not a mental abstraction, it is relative to life and must be reconcilable with feeling. As an instance of the difficulties which confront the head-heart relationship Fletcher gives the case of Christian humility. The lowly, contrite and loving heart can understand the paradox of a humility that grows as the soul grows: the understanding cannot comprehend it, but yet in Christian experience, finds it to be not irrational.[32]

IV. PRE-REQUISITES FOR GROWTH IN GRACE

From Fletcher's account of the scope of piety we turn to consider how the soul actually moves towards the accomplishment of its aim. The material for this part of our study is nowhere neatly arranged by Fletcher himself, but the pattern of his thought is clear enough.

He teaches that there are three spiritual pre-requisites without which holiness as he understood it is impossible. These are humility, expectation, and resignation. When we speak of them as pre-requisites it is not to imply that they exist only to prepare for something else, but to indicate their primary importance in the spiritual life. They could be called fundamental principles of sanctity.

[30] *Works*, VII.466.   [31] Cf. ibid. II.210-11.   [32] Ibid. p. 367.

As far as we can see, they are permanent human attitudes. There is no sanctity, here on earth at any rate, which can outgrow them or dispense with them. In some ways they correspond to 'style' in art or athletics, being largely unselfconscious and habitual. They are not the flower of accomplishment, although like seeds they are unfolded in growth.

(1) *Humility*

'Before honour is humility,' says Fletcher in a passage on man's lamentable blindness and helplessness.[33] Humility is the attitude that springs from a true understanding of God and self. It is not simply the absence of pride. It is a positive quality or grace, which bows in the presence of God and which leads the soul to acknowledge itself the chief of sinners.[34] Fletcher ranks it with charity as one of the capital graces without which religion, no matter how organized, is a soul-less form.[35] It is the very antithesis of pharisaism, and Fletcher thinks of pharisaism as the 'proud gigantic mind' that cannot stoop as Christ did in the meekness and lowliness of His earthly ministry.

This grace is the door to Christian spirituality, and it is the door through which all must pass. Fletcher says explicitly that 'Perfect humility [is] the grace which is most essential to the perfect Christian's character.'[36] 'Penitential poverty of spirit,' which is a favourite definition of humility with Fletcher, is, he says, 'the first commandment of Christ's evangelical law.'[37] Without humility, neither understanding, nor will, nor affections can be redeemed. Without it truth cannot be known, nor self-will rectified, nor the divine love felt. No matter whether Christian spirituality be thought of in terms of the vision of God, fellowship with God, or as virtuous character, these are possible only to the man who is of a humble

[33] Ibid. II.162. [34] Cf. ibid. pp. 366-7. [35] Ibid. VIII.204.
[36] Ibid. VI.324. [37] Ibid. p. 331.

and contrite mind. Before a man can enjoy spiritual health he must acknowledge that there is no health in himself.

Fletcher's stress upon humility is heavy, but he retains his customary balance. If 'humility' is a capital grace, 'voluntary humility' is a deadly sin. The phrase comes from Colossians 2^{18}. Wesley, as well as Fletcher, used it frequently to express the notion of self-abasement to the point of debility. It connotes self-distrust without trust in God, the spirit which acknowledges that in the self dwelleth no good thing without going on to say 'by faith all things are possible'. The phrase has other complexions. It sometimes indicates reluctance to push on in the spiritual life for fear of 'presumption',[38] and again, a dangerous refinement of humility itself which leads Christians to query why God has been pleased to reveal his grace in them.[39]

The view that some remains of sin is a good thing in Christians in order to keep them humble finds in Fletcher a relentless enemy. 'Who has more sin than Satan?', he raps out, 'and who is prouder?' No, the evangelical method of obtaining this grace is 'to look at Christ in the manger, in Gethsemane, or on the Cross; to consider him when he washes his disciples' feet; and obediently to listen to him when he says Learn of me for I am meek and lowly in heart.'[40]

(2) *Expectation (or Hope)*

The second human quality, or 'virtue', to use theological language, without which growth into Perfection is impossible, is, properly speaking, 'hope'. Because this term is rarely used in its New Testament sense, and indeed often implies a doubt, we will keep to the term 'Expectation'. Fletcher frequently employed the word. This virtue is, in fact, a combination of Faith and Hope. It is

[38] *Works*, II.187.   [39] Ibid. p. 234.   [40] Ibid. VI.145.

the firm, sustained conviction that God is leading the soul on in the life of grace.

Fletcher sometimes had difficulty with his penitents of persuading them that the highest expectations are not inconsistent with the lowliest humility. To balance these two effectively was one of the major problems of Fletcher's controversial *Works*. He wrote to Charles Wesley on the subject saying: 'I wish we could find the right way of reconciling the most profound humility with the most lively hopes of grace.'[41]

So important is the spirit of expectation that Fletcher calls it the first of the inward means of grace. The soul must believe that God can, and expect that he will perform his promises, that he is willing and able to manifest himself to the believer as he does not to the world. 'This', says Fletcher, 'is the very root of prayer, fervency, hope and expectation. Without the actings of this preparatory faith, the soul droops and becomes an easy prey to despondency, vanity, or sloth. Where this talent is buried the Lord seldom works. "Believest thou that I am able to do this for thee?" is generally the first question he puts to the seeker's heart. If it be answered in the negative, he can do no great miracle, because of this unbelief.'[42] Fletcher admits that sometimes God breaks in upon men where there is no expectation, but this fact in no wise invalidates the principle that growth in holiness is impossible without expectation of spirit.

(3) *Resignation*

The humility that looks up for all that the soul needs in its pilgrimage towards perfection, and the lively expectation that God will supply those needs, must be matched by complete resignation to the divine Will as to how this takes place. Fletcher has more to say on this subject, perhaps, than upon any other aspect of the spiritual life.

[41] Ibid. VII.388.   [42] Ibid. VII.347-8.

This is understandable. In actual life, with its pain, sickness, sorrow, accident, misfortune—all that the flesh is heir to—the inability to endure is the scene of most spiritual wrecks. Concerning what Fletcher calls 'the Spiritual Manifestation of the Son of God' he insists that we must be absolutely resigned to God as to the manner, time and place in which God deals with us. It is so in everything. Fletcher writes 'Through patience [one aspect of resignation], as well as faith and prayer, we inherit the blessing. Some, according to their carnal wisdom and forward imagination, mark out the way in which salvation is to come to their hearts; but the Lord generally disappoints these unhumbled seekers.'[43]

Sanctification, Fletcher taught, 'is not generally the work of a day, nor of a year . . . it is in general a progressive work, and of long duration'.[44] Apart from the inner struggle, the soul is beset by temptations and trials. Resignation alone brings peace and fruitfulness to the soul in such conditions. 'Absolute resignation to the divine Will', he writes, 'baffles a thousand temptations, confidence in our Saviour carries us sweetly through a thousand trials.'[45]

Fletcher has not left detailed writing about temptation. Like Wesley, he states the necessity of not continuing in any known sin. Humility, expectation and resignation free the soul from self-consciousness in its holiness. The meticulous weighing of or worrying about one's sin (itself a sin, i.e. 'scrupulosity' in technical language) finds no place in the sincere soul governed by the three prerequisites we have named.

Concerning 'trials' Fletcher has much to say. Trials, of course, may be temptations also. But by the term Fletcher means such things as sickness, bereavement, old age, affliction, personal sorrow, change of circumstances, and so on. The resignation of a Christian under such trials is

[43] *Works*, VII.348.   [44] Ibid. p. 305.   [45] Ibid. I.228.

SAINT

supernatural, not stoical. To a sick man who was desirous to be up and about on the Lord's work, Fletcher wrote: 'If I were by you I would preach to your heart and my own, a lecture on that text, We are saved by hope, and by a faith which is never stronger than when it is contrary to all the feelings of flesh and blood.' And later on in that same letter he reiterates: 'Nothing enlarges the heart and awakens the soul more than believing, loving expectation. Let us wait together until we are all endued with power from on high.'[46]

Fletcher's spiritual teaching holds this trinity—humility, expectation and resignation together. Though distinguishable in thought, they all qualify each other. Thus, humble, expectant resignation, averts peevishness, murmuring, complaining, ingratitude, evil-reasoning and such-like, whatever our lot. It strangles that parent of so much spiritual disorder—the self-pitying query: 'Why has this happened to me?'[47]

That rare spirit of Christian detachment is begotten by this trinity. Fletcher exemplified this great paradox of being able to enter into and to use earthly things, relationships, circumstances with the intensity of spiritual purpose, and yet of being ready to surrender them without loss at the divine behest. Behind this resignation, of course, lies the doctrine of Providence. In another letter to the sick lady previously mentioned, he wrote: 'If a sparrow falleth not to the ground, nor a hair from our heads without our Father's leave, it is certain that the higher circumstances of our life are planned by the wise and gracious Governor of all things. This kind of faith in Providence I find of indispensable necessity to go calmly through life, and, I think, through death also.'[48] Such detachment growing in the soil of humility, expectation and resignation, promotes and sustains service for humanity. This also is a Christian paradox. Fletcher

[46] Ibid. I.312-13. [47] Cf. ibid. VII.410. [48] Ibid. VII.412.

expresses it characteristically thus: 'In being moderate, humble and truly desirous to be a Christian, that is to be the least, the last, and the servant of all, we avoid running into difficulties. We escape many temptations, and many mortifying disappointments. For my part, as I expect nothing from men they cannot disappoint me; and as I expect all things from God in the time, way, measure and manner it pleaseth him to bestow, here I cannot be disappointed because he does and will do all things well.'[49]

V. THE CULTIVATION OF THE SPIRITUAL LIFE

Fletcher himself did not often speak about cultivating the spiritual life, but as a master of that life, and as a director of souls his writings abound in practical counsels to 'professors', i.e. to serious Christians who avowed themselves as such. This term 'professors' was Revival-speech. It was not so formal as it may sound today, although it did indicate almost always, membership in some group or society existing to promote vital religion. Spiritual guidance and sustenance in these groups often came from the Evangelical Revival literature, amongst which Fletcher's *Works* were highly rated. Not that we find guide-book precision there. All the same, the harmony of his spiritual directions is clear enough to set down in print under the several headings which follow.

(1) *Contemplative and Active Elements*

It is probable that a religion of absolute spirituality is impossible here on earth. Certainly, Christian spirituality has its inward and its outward aspects, which are inseparably joined in human experience, although the extent of each, and the emphasis placed upon each, may vary considerably.

As a spiritual director Fletcher sanely holds a balance between the contemplative and active; in his own life

[49] *Works*, VII p. 474.

also both elements are intense, so that on occasion we feel that he is essentially a mystic, and then at other times we want to say that he believes in 'salvation by works'.

In a spiritual letter full of characteristic allusions written to Henry Brooke, we find Fletcher firmly pleading for the vital partnership of both elements. 'You are certainly right', he says, 'when you prefer the inward to the outward; the former is the safer, but both together make up the beauty of holiness. The inward life may be compared to the husband, the outward to the fruitful wife. What God hath joined together, let no man, nor even angel put asunder. . . . To wait in deep resignation and with a constant attention to what the Lord will please to do, or say, concerning us and his Church; and to leave to him the times and the seasons, is what I am chiefly called to do; taking care in the meanwhile of falling into either ditch: I mean into *speculation* which is careless of action, or into the *activity* which is devoid of spirituality. I would not have a lamp without oil, and I could not have oil without a lamp, and a vessel to hold it in for myself, and to communicate it to others.'[50]

When in this letter he gives priority to the inward aspects of religion, he means that man's holiness has its origin and its sublimest moments in the operation of the divine Spirit. This is expressed in a variety of ways. For instance, he wrote: 'The sun shines, not because we deserve it by undrawing our curtains, but because it is its nature. Jesus visits us, not because of any merit in our prayers, etc., but for his own sake, because his truth and compassions fail not.'[51] At other times, Fletcher expresses this truth in terms of Sanctification proper, as when he wrote to his parishioners saying: 'This indwelling of the Comforter perfects the mystery of sanctification in the believer's soul. This is the highest blessing of the

[50] Ibid. VII.468-9.   [51] Ibid. p. 350.

Christian Covenant on earth.' This is immediate communion with God.[52]

Outward instruction is of value, and so Fletcher does his utmost to secure the best possible curate for his parishioners, but he reminds them that whatever happens in that direction, they have an Inward Instructor to whom they must attend.[53] Occasionally he defends mysticism, by which he means the ability to 'fathom the deep mysteries of inward religion',[54] although he recognizes the dangers of mysticism of William Law's type.[55] Still he urges the possibility and the reality of a depth of prayer, which 'comes within reach of the internal world', and once employed mystical language proper in speaking of the supreme religious experience as 'the beatific vision'. Incidentally, it is the humblest men who long most for this.[56]

(2) *The Means of Grace*

The phrase, 'the means of grace' became familiar speech in Methodist circles to indicate the ordinary ways by which grace is ministered to the soul. The expression often carried an emphasis upon the characteristic provisions of Methodism, such as attending the preaching or class meeting. Fletcher, like Wesley, used the expression in the full sense of the Church's Canons which enjoin use of both outward and inward ways of religion. Fletcher's intensity of personal piety and public ministry does not go beyond his ordination vow nor beyond Canon XIII. This states: 'All manner of persons within the Church of England shall from henceforth celebrate and keep the Lord's Day, commonly called Sunday, and other holydays according to God's holy will and pleasure, and the orders of the Church of England prescribed in that behalf, that is, in hearing the word of God read and taught; in

---

[52] *Works*, I.224; cf. VII.360-1.   [53] Ibid. I.201.
[54] Ibid. III.172.   [55] Ibid. II.356.   [56] Ibid. VI.289.

private and public prayers; in acknowledging their offence to God, and amendment of the same; in reconciling themselves charitably to their neighbours where displeasure hath been; in oftentimes receiving the Communion of the body and blood of Christ; in visiting of the poor and sick; using all godly and sober conversation.'

(a) *The Public Means of Grace.* In the General Thanksgiving we are taught to be grateful for 'the means of grace'. Bishop Reynolds of Norwich, the author of that prayer, probably had uppermost in mind the whole liturgical provision of the Book of Common Prayer. In Chapter 2 we noted Fletcher's high regard for the Liturgy. Here we need to note that Fletcher's own piety was established on the basis of that Liturgy. Few of his parishioners, probably, joined with him in the daily offices, but the value of this discipline was known and accepted by many Anglican Methodists. Holy souls rejoiced in the privilege of regular Communion. The more mystical the soul's experience, the greater the proficiency in interior prayer, the more necessary it is to submit to the public worship of the Church.

In the most mystical of all Fletcher's *Works*—his *Spiritual Manifestation*—he yet asserts the wisdom of the Church's discipline. He writes: 'These means are both outward and inward. The outward are what our Church calls "The Means of grace", particularly hearing or reading the word, partaking of the sacraments, and praying together with one accord for the manifestation of the Spirit, as the primitive Christians did. Those means are to be used with the greatest diligence, but not to be trusted to; the only proper object of our confidence is God, who works all in all.'[57]

The most evangelical religion also needs a social discipline. 'Attend a plain, heartsearching ministry as often as possible; and when the sword of the spirit, the

[57] Ibid. VII.347.

word of God, pierces thy soul, beware of fretful impatience. Instead of rising with indignation against the preacher ... account him thy best friend that wounds the deepest, provided he bring thee to Christ for a cure.'[58]

(*b*) *Private Means of Grace.* Alongside the public means of grace are those which the Church leaves to the initiative of the Ministry or to that of its lay-people. For some there is formal provision. Others, auricular confession, for instance, are permissive. The troubled mind or conscience may freely open up its grief to the parish priest, 'or to some other discreet and learned minister of God's word'.[59] Methodist class and band meetings, as well as less organized meetings for prayer ('social prayer' he often called it) were encouraged by Fletcher as means to growth in Christian character and experience. It was not good for even the holiest of men 'to eat his morsel alone'. There is deep psychological as well as theological justification for Fletcher's insistence upon that.

Fletcher rated 'spiritual counsel' very highly amongst the private means of grace. The extent to which this was employed in eighteenth-century religion is not generally realized today. But those who have studied the diaries and intimate biographies of the period know that spiritual direction had an important place in Wesley's Methodist provision for serious Christians. Fletcher was guide to many fine as well as simple souls. He puts the case thus: 'As soon as we discover our spiritual blindness, we mistrust our own judgement, feel the need of instruction, modestly repair to the experienced for advice, carefully search the Scriptures, readily follow their blessed directions and fervently pray that no false light may mislead us out of the way of salvation.'[60]

The need for this guidance is not confined only to the beginning of the spiritual life, or to so-called practical

[58] *Works*, II.172. [59] Exhortation, Communion Office (1662).
[60] *Works*, II.162.

matters such as 'changing one's estate' (getting married) or taking up a new occupation. Humility deepens as the soul matures so that the best of saints needs his confessor.

Although the soul is not saved by works, it cannot be saved without them. These, although commanded by the Church, are left largely to the individual's own discretion —unless they are enjoined by a director. 'All divines agree', writes Fletcher, 'that good works are of three sorts: 1. Works of piety towards God; 2. Works of charity towards our neighbour; and 3. Works of self denial towards ourselves.' Only those which fall in the second and third classes can be called private means of grace. The Christian grows in grace, says Fletcher, when he does good to the souls and bodies of men.

A large part of each man's life is private, both in the sense that it is interior and in that it is self-determined. But Fletcher allows no dual standard. The Christian has always to subdue the flesh and to 'take up his cross'. The chief means to the former are given as 'moderate use of meat, drink and sleep; self-denial in apparel, furniture and equipage; chastity in all its branches; subduing our slothful, rebellious flesh by early rising, abstinence, fasting; and, in a word, by taking up our daily cross, and following our abstemious and yet laborious Lord.'[61] Every duty, even worldly business in an uncongenial sphere,[62] must, under God, become the soil in which the fruit of holiness is produced. There is no place in Fletcher for withdrawal from the world.[63]

(3) *The Religious Vocation*

We have culled from Fletcher's writings, a body of holy wisdom in which the aims and principles of the spiritual life are revealed. The essential nature of that life is supernatural, producing human character of self-evidencing

[61] Ibid. IV.77. [62] Cf. ibid. VII.451. [63] Ibid. II.176.

value and beauty. But, as no one can tell another how to respond the divine motions within, the soul which desires this holiness and looks for the way thereto, will be conscious of a certain loneliness at first. Each soul must accept its vocation in responsibility to God alone, and work its own way in the mysterious fellowship with the divine spirit. This is reflected in the sublime courtesy with which Fletcher deals with his spiritual children. Even when he is most passionate, when his spiritual counsel runs in the moulds of rhetoric, he touches the soul with the utmost delicacy, though with firmness.

Who are called to this vocation? Fletcher would have considered this an easy question. Every Christian is called to be a saint. Fletcher shows no sympathy with attempts to encourage the professional religious, and gives not the slightest hint of accepting a double standard. The intensity of spiritual culture which he expects the ordinary Christian to be capable of is a striking thing. He writes very often as though there were nothing else on earth but religion. He calls his parishioners to a devotion which many people imagine to be possible only in a religious order of the enclosed kind.

It must be admitted that his evangelicalism sometimes shows a negative attitude to secular life. He does not hold that it is unredeemed, of course, or irredeemable. In his catechetical instruction he urged that duty be done in that state of life into which it shall please God to call us. But secular life is rather a cross to be endured than a calling to be enjoyed. Perhaps his most forthright expression of this outlook occurs in a comment upon the parable of the talents, where he says: 'Now the non-improvement of a natural talent, suppose for poetry or husbandry can never constitute a man *wicked*, nothing can do this but the non-improvement of a talent of grace.'[64] He is on safer ground when he instructs earnest seekers 'to take care not to

[64] *Works*, IV.439.

SAINT

mistake gifts for graces; fluency of speech for converting power; the warmth of natural affection for divine love; or the impulse of God's spirit on some particular occasion for an evidence of spiritual regeneration'.[65] But the mere possibility of such confusion indicates the proximity of the earthly and the heavenly.

Over against Fletcher's narrower evangelicalism, however, must be set his teaching on the four points which follow, viz.:

(a) *Degrees of Light.* Although God visits all men so as to strive with them and reprove them, yet there are degrees of the manifestation of the spirit.[66] All men are called to the life of truth and love, but those who do not respond to the Spirit can never rise above the life of the flesh. But Fletcher will have none of the narrowness which says: 'Toe the line with us or be doomed.' Although he does not carefully work out the stages of the soul's progress except in the broadest outline, or catalogue differences of spiritual attainment, he deplores the sheep-and-goat classification. In a piece of irony upon animalistic metaphors for humanity he soliloquizes: 'But I am a little embarrassed. If none go to hell but *goats*, and none go to heaven but *sheep*, where shall the *chickens* go? Where the *wolves in sheep's clothing?* And in what limbus of heaven or hell shall be put that fox *Herod*, the *dogs* who *return to their vomit*, and the *swine* before whom we must *not cast our pearls*: are they all species of goats or some particular kind of sheep?'[67] To the objection that a man must either be in a state of enmity with God, or a state of pardon or reconciliation Fletcher rejoins: 'What, Sir! Is there no medium between these extremes? There is, as surely as the morning dawn intervenes between midnight and noonday.'[68]

(b) *Growth and Conversion.* Holiness has its laws of growth

---

[65] Ibid. II.175. [66] Ibid. III.56-7.
[67] Ibid. p. 40 (Fletcher's italics). [68] Ibid. III.57.

just as the natural world has. The degrees of the Spirit's manifestation have their counterpart in the degrees of human apprehension and response. Fletcher does not expect men to 'leap at once to the middle, much less to the highest round' of the ladder of truth. The most sudden conversions, he goes on to say, imply a gradual transition. The soul must take the steps within its reach before it can mount to maturity.[69]

(c) *Secondary Motives for Holiness.* Fletcher's Calvinist opponents deplored the place he gave to activity in the spiritual life; they dubbed it 'working for life'. Fletcher maintained his enlightened self-interest doctrine as reasonable, wise and scriptural. Against Molinos, Madame Guyon and Fénelon (in his early ministry) Fletcher holds that secondary motives such as punishment here and hell hereafter, as well as fear of God, the promise of future rewards, and a well-ordered self-love are proper motives for holiness, even though they be secondary. It is voluntary humility, i.e. spurious humility to despise the divine promise of peace, happiness and glory.[70] Mystical aberrations such as 'stillness' have no place in Fletcher's teaching.

(d) *Conformity to Custom in things Indifferent.* Singularity is no necessary concomitant of holiness. When John Wesley said 'Be singular or be damned' he was speaking of spiritual distinction, not of indifferent matters of dress or personal habit. Fletcher advised people to dress suitably to their station and rank. He did not recommend any holy demeanour. 'There is no sin in looking cheerful,' he wrote to Miss Hatton, although he added that she must distinguish between cheerfulness and levity. He continues: 'Beware of stiff singularity in things barely indifferent—it is self in disguise; and it is so much the more dangerous, as it comes recommended by a serious, self-denying, religious appearance.'[71]

[69] *Works*, IV.162.   [70] Ibid. pp. 99, 128ff.   [71] Ibid. VII.402.

The religious vocation is one of great seriousness, but not one of gloomy sorrow. The serious Christian must beware of dissipation, he must shun diversions, amusements, bodily indulgence entangling the affections, too much sleep and conviviality. He must also avoid the hurry of business as much as possible.[72]

On the other hand Fletcher taught that recollectedness is possible even in the hurry of business. He urges reasonableness even in spiritual exercises. He tells his people to beware of struggling against the secondary causes of life, i.e. against one's environment and lot. He bids them not to work themselves up into any artificial frames, say of anguish. Such moods as impatience, discontent, sullenness, must be driven out. The soul must be self-possessed; it must cultivate the amiability of faith.[73]

Fletcher recognized that there must be ups and downs in the spiritual life. 'The weeping frame of repentance' and that of joyous faith are 'happily mixed', he writes to Lady Mary Fitzgerald. There is nothing in Fletcher that corresponds to the teaching of the mystics regarding the 'dark night of the soul'. He does, indeed, speak of winter periods in the soul and in the ministry; but the soul may bear the fruit of holiness all the year round. Like Wesley, Fletcher does not believe that God withdraws his presence from the covenanted soul; such dry periods as the soul may experience cannot amount to dereliction.[74]

(4) *The Practice of Holiness*

In Fletcher's teaching there are no rule-of-thumb methods, but on the other hand, there is nothing hazy or doubtful. Fletcher epitomizes his own teaching as follows: 'The sum of all I have preached to you is contained in the

[72] Cf. ibid. II.173. [73] Cf. ibid. I.94, II.166-7.
[74] Cf. ibid. III.135, VII.410.

following four propositions. First, heartily repent of your sins, original and actual. Secondly, believe the gospel of Christ in sincerity and truth. Thirdly, in the power which true faith gives (for all things *commanded* are possible to him that believeth) run with humble confidence the way of God's commandments before God and man. Fourthly, by continuing to take up your cross, and to receive the pure milk of God's word, grow in grace and in the knowledge of Jesus Christ.'[75] That is a perfect account of every complete act of turning to God after sin, i.e. of contrition, as well as a nutshell summary of the soul's pilgrimage at large.

The mention of contrition leads us to the question of sins and how to deal with them. Whilst Fletcher does not comprehensively catalogue these, nor give meticulous directions concerning them, he never falls into the bland piety that can confess to 'sin' and yet not deal with actual sins. No Roman moral theologian could surpass him in analysing human sinfulness. For instance, in his *Appeal*. Thinking only in terms of individual experience, he mentions in one breath, the following unholy moods and tempers—pride, independence, ambition, vanity, sloth, envy, covetousness, impatience, wrath, malice, jealousy, idolatrous love, hatred, revenge, hypocrisy, bigotry, perfidiousness, despair and distraction. Then he cries out: 'And are your hearts, O ye sons of men, the favourite seat of this infernal crew? Then shame on the wretch that made the first panegyric on the dignity of human nature! He proved my point: he began in Pride, and ended in Distraction.'[76]

The Christian, however, in Fletcher's teaching is not to be preoccupied with sin, nor is he to concentrate upon it. Fletcher quotes approvingly a passage from John Newton which draws a distinction between sins and infirmities.[77] This distinction, based upon the definition of sin as a

[75] *Works*, I.219-20.   [76] Ibid. II.75.   [77] Ibid. VI.312.

voluntary transgression of a known law, is that which is expressed theologically in the terms 'mortal sin' and 'venial sin'. Fletcher did not use these terms, probably from fear of antinomian consequences and horror of Roman misuses. Without some such distinction, however, the awakened soul would be bowed down with intolerable scrupulosity and hopelessness.

In spiritual wisdom, as in the wisdom of common life, prevention is better than cure. Fletcher, like all the masters, taught that the soul which knows itself and values its peace, will cultivate those graces and that temper which will keep it occupied but not hurried, watchful but not morbid, joyful but not dissipated, recollected but not remote from men and affairs.

Fletcher's spirituality does not ignore the human body. But in this matter his precepts were sounder than his own practice. He acknowledged 'the close connection between the soul and the body, and that each has a reciprocal influence upon the other'. He grants that 'a cheerful mind is conducive to bodily health' and that a sluggish or sick or decaying body presses down the soul and may even overpower it.[78] In this extremity the soul would no longer be accountable, but in all other cases, the soul aided by divine grace, is considered capable of gaining the victory. As with most spiritual directors, Fletcher was much harder on himself than upon his penitents. Fasting is enjoined by the Church, but he issues a warning against excessive fasting and the hard usages of the body practised by some Roman Catholics.[79] Incidentally, the work in which this advice is given, namely, the *Concluding Address*, is a little classic of spiritual direction, full of the maturest and most practical holy wisdom.

Before leaving the subject of the body, a word may be said about the spiritual significance of dreams. Long before theories of the subconscious gained attention

[78] Ibid. V.416.   [79] Ibid. II.176.

Fletcher, and Wesley also, insisted that Christian spirituality would make our very dreams devout. In a little document giving headings for self-examination, the twentieth runs—'How am I in my sleep? If Satan presents an evil imagination does my will immediately resist or give way to it?'[80] That is a thoroughly scientific test of spiritual health.

In spite of all that has been said in this book concerning reason, sanity and balance, it remains that the spiritual life is mysterious, and largely interior. Mrs Fletcher lamented the fact that her husband left no account of his mystical experiences. When she said that 'he acted and spoke and thought as under the eye of God. And thus he remained unmoved in all occurrences, at all times and on every occasion possessing inward recollection',[81] she knew that it was because he had passed, in words which he sometimes quoted from the seventeenth-century English mystic, Thomas Bromley, 'from the outward to the inward and from the inward to the inmost'.[82]

Interior spirituality, whilst drawing sustenance from all the means of grace, must be cultivated particularly in the spirit of watchfulness and recollection. God must be sought by shutting out the sensuous as much as possible, and by patient waiting for that communion with Him which can be felt and recognized. In order to enjoy this most fruitful of all fellowships Fletcher encourages a method of acts of devotion of a mental kind.

Watchfulness is essential for two main reasons; first, because without it the soul falls an easy victim to sins of surprise, and secondly, because of the ancient enmity between the flesh and the spirit. As Fletcher put it: 'More ships of war are destroyed by worms than by shots of the enemy.'[83]

Hard upon watchfulness in the practice of holiness

---

[80] *Works*, VIII.431. [81] Ibid. I.394.
[82] Ibid. VII.469. [83] Ibid. VIII.198.

follows recollectedness. This makes the soul 'all eye, all ear'. Fletcher sums up its value under seven headings:

(1) It secures quietness so that God can be heard.
(2) 'It is the altar on which we must offer up our Isaacs.'
(3) It is a ladder to God.
(4) It centres the soul upon God, its true centre.
(5) It is the holy of holies in the human temple.
(6) It uncovers heaven in the heart.
(7) Without it the means of grace are useless, or at best superficial.[84]

All acts of devotion must take place in this spirit. In this spirit all the soul's needs, reflections, aspirations and moods may be spread before God. For instance, self-examination, although a necessity, will only be safe if it is undertaken as an act of the recollected soul. Any spiritual lack may be considered and named in such an act, and passionately desired not merely passively prayed for.

A pattern for such an act of devotion is given to his correspondent Miss Hatton: 'Love is the passion [in her case at that time] which wants to be stirred: do it with all calmness—"I *will* love him, I *do* love him a *little*, I shall love him *much*, because he has first loved me, etc." '[85] He instructs her further to make frequent acts of desire, resignation, reliance, faith, and so on. In short, she is to meet Christ in her heart by simple recollection. That is the secret of holiness and the source of the peace and joy which are beyond the understanding.

What Fletcher taught, he practised, and when he is reflective, we see that his experience is the best validation of his teaching. To his friend James Ireland he opened up his heart thus: 'The Lord teaches me four lessons; the first is to be *thankful* that I am out of hell; the second to be *nothing* before him; the third to *receive* the gift of God—

[84] Ibid. I.95. [85] Ibid. VII.414.

the person of Jesus; and the fourth to feel my want of the *Spirit* of Jesus and to wait for it. These four lessons are very deep: O when shall I have learned them? Let us go together to the School of Jesus, and learn to be meek and lowly in heart. Adieu.'[86]

---

[86] *Works*, I.176-7.

Conclusion

FLETCHER's life and work reveal a wonderful consistency. Humility, sincerity, honesty, fearlessness, single-mindedness and holy calmness shine all the way through. To follow his romantic life, to see him at his canonical duty, to pick up the pages beneath his controversial pen, to study his theology, and sympathetically to approach his sanctity, is to discover the golden thread of that consistency, which is the Truth and Love of God in Jesus Christ.

These awoke him in his early days. They determined his creed and governed his ecclesiastical loyalties. They evoked his most virile literary style. He cherished them in his 'hermitage' and in every act of devotion. He yearned to share them pastorally, and to express them to all with whom he had to do.

Whatever seraphic marks he bore upon his body, he surely bore the marks of the Lord Jesus upon his ministry and sanctity. As the saints are not in competition they probably abhor comparisons. But without odium we may wonder why this St John is not canonized more in the hearts of Anglicans and Methodists, and indeed of all who sing of Truth and Love.

For our last flaming glimpse of the Shropshire Saint let us turn to the conclusion of the *Essay on Truth*.[1] In the quietness of a tiny study little bigger than a monk's cell, forgetful of the fact that his kitchen was denuded of its pewter, and even of food—in order to feed God's poor, he writes upon his knees, with tears of faith and hope and love upon his cheeks:

[1] Ibid. IV.232-3.

'O Jesus, stand by our weakness and we will stand by thy truth. Thou sayest, Will ye also go away? And to whom should we go, Gracious Lord? Hast thou not the words of Truth, the words of everlasting life? Art thou not the light of the world and the light of men? Our light and life? Could all the ignes fatui in the professing world; could all the stars in thy church, supply the want of thy light to our souls? No, Lord; Be then our sun and shield for ever. Visit the earth again, thou uncreated Sun of righteousness and truth; hasten thy second advent: Thy kingdom come! Shine without a cloud! Scatter the last remains of error's night! Kindle our minds into pure truth! our hearts into perfect love! our tongues into ardent praise! our lives into flaming obedience!'

> *Bold may we wax, exceeding bold,*
> *No more to Error's ways conform,*
> *Nor shrink the hardest Truths t' unfold,*
> *But more than meet the gathering storm.*
>
> *Adverse to earth's erroneous throng,*
> *May each now turn his fearless face:*
> *Stand as an iron pillar strong,*
> *And steadfast as a wall of brass.*
>
> *Give us thy might, thou God of pow'r,*
> *Then let or men or fiends assail:*
> *Strong in thy strength, we'll stand a tow'r,*
> *Impregnable to earth or hell.*

Index

Active element in piety, 116-18
Acts, of devotion, etc., 129
Address to Earnest Seekers, 40-1
Adjectives, 40, 58-9, 88
Affective piety, 107-10
à Kempis, Thomas, 4, 12
Allegory, 37, 40, 60-1, 80, 105
Allen, Margaret, vii, ix
American Patriotism, xv, 92
Anglicanism, 20ff, 96
Answer to Toplady's Vindication of the Decrees, xv, 72
Anthony of Padua, 39
Antinomianism, 58, 67, 69, 87, 100, 103
Aphorism, 37, 61-2
Apostrophe, 64
Appeal to Matter of Fact, xv, 39, 40, 53, 83, 97
Architecture and Anglican Worship, 29-30
Aquinas, Thomas, 75, 103
Arminian, -ism, x, 70, 103
Articles, Thirty-nine, 30, 73
Ashton and Sykes: *Coal Industry*, 3
Athanasian Creed, 28, 80
Atonement, 85
Attingham House (Tern Hall), 4
Augustine, 98

Balance, Fletcher's, 69, 108, 112, 113, 116
Baptism, 21, 30, 81, 86, 101
Baptist Meeting, 17
Baxter, Richard, x, 35
Bengelius, 78
Benson, Joseph, vii, viii, xiii, xvi, xvii, 11, 36, 39
Beveridge, Bishop, 70
Biblicist, Fletcher as, 78
Bidding Prayer, 24
Bluntness, Fletcher's Helvetic, 8, 17, 27
Body, the human, 127
Bosanquet, Mary (Mrs Fletcher), ix, xii, xiii, 11, 128
Bourne, Hugh, xv
Bridgnorth, vii, 34

Bromley, Thomas, 128
Brooke family of Madeley, 15
Brooke, Henry, 117
Brown, Joseph, 106
Bucer, Martin, 74
Bunyan, John, 60, 61
Burials, Sunday, 22
Burns, J., vii, ix

Calvinism, x, 6, 11, 69, 84-5, 91, 100, 103
Canons, The, 24, 74, 118
Catholic Thought, 97, 102
Charity, 25, 97-9
Charles I., 30
Checks, Fletcher's, xv, 34, 67, 68, 73, 99
Children, education of, 26
Fletcher and, 9
Church Pastoral Aid Society, viii
Churchmanship, Fletcher's, 28-30, 92
Claridge, Richard, 19
Class Meetings, 21, 120
Clergy, 22
Coal, 2
Coalbrookdale, 1, 3, 17
Coalport, 1
Colloquialisms, 37, 55
Common Prayer, Book of, 22, 28-30, 41, 119
Compound adjectives, nouns, etc., 59, 60
Concluding Address, 127
Conference, Methodist, xii, 7
Conscience, 79
Contemplation, 116-18
Contrition, 126
Controversy, 11, 37-8, 57, 66, 68
Conversion, 4, 6, 31, 86, 123
Counsel, spiritual, 120
Court, *Rise of Midland Industries*, 3
Cox, Robert, vii, viii, 31, 34-5
Cranage, George, 19
Cranmer, Thomas, 20, 70
Crisp, Dr, 48, 17
Custom, 124

D'Ars, Curé, 96
Da Vinci, 1
Daily Office, 30
Darby, Abiah, 18-19
  Family, 15
Death, 104
Desk, the, 29
Detachment, 115
Dialogue, 40, 57, 58
Discourse on New Birth, xvi
Dispensations, the various, 89-91, 93
Doctrine, xi, 80-1
Double-standard, 121
Dreadful Phenomenon, xv, 33
Dreams, 4, 127-8
Duty, Clerical, 23

Election, doctrine of, 6
Elizabethan Settlement, 20
Emotion, 107-8
Emotive language, 64, 107
England, 6, 8, 9
Enthymeme, 76
Epictetus, 83
Equal Check, xv, 23, 39, 57, 58, 70, 79, 80, 89
Erasmus, 74
Eschatology, 93-4
Evangelical, -ism, 56, 82ff., 88, 100, 101, 111, 112, 122-3
Evangelical, Conception of the, 88-9
Evans, Caleb, 38
Expectation in piety, 112-13, 115
Eyton's *Antiquities of Shropshire*, 3

Faith, 4, 38, 85, 87, 102, 112
Fall, doctrine of, 82-3
Fasting, 30, 121, 127
Fénelon, 124
Fictitious and Genuine Creed, xv, 37
Fire of London, collection after, 13
Fitzgerald, Lady Mary, 105, 109, 125
Fletcher, J., vii
Fletcher, Mrs., *see* Bosanquet, Mary
Freedom, human, 84-5

Geneva, 4, 60, 85, 96
Gilpin, Joshua, ix
God, epithets for, 81-2
Goodwin, John, 68
Grace, 90

Grammar, 62
Greaves (Fletcher's Curate), 23
Gregory, Benjamin, viii
Growth, spiritual, 110, 114, 121, 123
Guyon, Madame, 124

Hatton, Miss, 124, 129
Haughmond Abbey, 4
Henry VIII, 13
Hereford, Bishop of, 1, 16
'Hermitage', Fletcher's, 14, 131
Hertfordshire, 3
Hiatt, Charles, 35
Hill family, the, 1
Hill, Richard, 67
Hill, Rowland, 11
History, 90-2, 93
Hobbes, 80, 84
Holy Communion, 27, 29, 119
Homilies, the, 30, 32, 73
Hooker, Richard, 74, 75
Hope, *see under* Expectation
Horace, 104
Horrible Decree, 6, 76
Hume, 80
Humility, grace of, 6, 110, 111-12, 121
Huntingdon, Lady, 10, 20, 24

Idiom, English, 40, 50ff., 54
Illustrations, Fletcher's, 61, 77, 98
Intellect, 103
Intention, 106
Inward aspects of piety, 116-17, 128
Ireland, James, 129
Iron, cast, 1, 2
Iron men, the, 1, 2
Ironbridge, 2, 3
Irony, 58, 64
Irregularity, Fletcher's, 24

Joy in religion, 110
Judiciousness, 68-9
Justification, 86, 87

La Louange (Poem), xvi, 35
Laud, William, 74
Law, William, 12, 118
Lectures (sermons), 23, 24
Lerins, Vincent de, 80
Letters, Fletcher's, 36-7

Liturgy, ix, 28-30, 32, 73, 74, 79, 119
Logic, 8, 64, 71, 76-7
Lord's prayer in liturgy, 29
Love, of God, of Christ, 4, 85, 103, 109, 131
Luther, Martin, 31, 74

Macdonald, F. W., vii, ix
Madeley bells, 15
  Chapelry, 13
  Church, 14-16
  Court, 15
  industries, 1-3
  Manor, 15
  parish, 7, 13, 14, 23, 25, 26
  population, 12
  vicarage, 14
Madeley Wood Chapel, 17
Marrat, J., vii, ix, 34
Marriage, Fletcher's, 12
Martindale, M., xvi
Martyr, Peter, 74
Means of grace, 118-21
Melanchthon, 31
Merit, 38
Metaphor, 55
Methodism, 4, 15, 21, 27, 107, 120
Methodists, 4, 6
Millenarianism, 93-4
Milton, John, 39
Ministry, Christian, 26, 31, 40
Miracle, 92
Molinos, 124
Montesquieu, 80
Motives, secondary, in piety, 124
Mysticism, xi, xii, 94, 118, 125, 128

Nature, 90
Necessity, 72, 84
Newcomen Society, Transactions of, 3
Newton, John, 126
Nouns, 88
Nowell, Alexander, 74
Nyon, 5

Occasional Offices, 26
Octagon, Madeley, 14, 15, 16
Open-air preaching, 22
Oratory, 32, 63
Orders, Presbyterian, 79
Ordination, Fletcher's, x, 5
Ordination charge, 26

Orthodoxy, 80-2
Outward aspects of piety, 117, 118
Oxford Dictionary of English Proverbs, 51-3
Oxford English Dictionary, 42-8, 63, 76

Parishioners, 21, 27, 122
Pastor, Fletcher as, 25ff.
Pelagianism, 69
Penance, 89
Perfection, 68, 99-101
Perronet, Edward and Miss, 94
Perseverance, 106
Philosopher, Fletcher as, 89-92
Plato, 104
Plymley, Archdeacon, 14
Poet, Fletcher as, 35
Polemical Essay, xv, 99
Politics, 92
Portrait of St Paul, xvi, 31, 40, 98
Prayer, 113, 119, 120
Preaching, Fletcher and, 30-3
Priest, Fletcher as, 27ff.
Priestley, Joseph, 80
Protestantism, 6, 17, 73-9
Proverbs, 40, 51-3
Providence, 72, 115
Pullan, Leighton, 66
Pulpit, 29

Quakers, 17, 18-20, 28, 86, 87
Quotation, interlarded, 78-9

Railton, Commissioner, ix
Rational Vindication of Catholic Faith, xvi, 41, 80
Reason, 8, 67, 75-7
Recollectedness in piety, 125, 129
Reformers, the, 20
Regeneration, 86
Reply to Principal Arguments, xvi
Reprobation, 90, 91
Resignation in piety, 113-16
Revelation, 90
Reynolds, Bishop, 119
Rhetoric, 40, 63-4
Rogers, James, 95
Roman Catholicism, 12, 17, 18, 79, 91, 109
Rose, Daniel, 19
Rousseau, 80
Ryle, Bishop J. C., vii, ix, x

Sacrament, the, 23, 24
Salopian Journal, 3
Sales, Francis de, 96
Salvationists, ix
Sanctification, xii, 81, 114, 117
Sangster, W. E., xii
Satan, 112
Satire, 56, 64
Scot, A., xvii
Scripture, 30, 40-1, 57, 77-9
Scripture Scales, xv, 39, 78
Scrupulosity, 114, 127
Scupoli, 96
Self-examination, 129
Sellon, Walter, 38
Seneca, 104
Sentences, length of, 63
Seriousness, 21, 36, 101
Sermons, 23, 24, 32, 33
Severn, River, 2, 3, 4
Sèvres ware, 1
Shakespeare, 11
Shrewsbury, 2, 4, 7
Shropshire, 3, 14
Sin, xii, 83, 84, 112, 114, 126
Sins, mortal and venial, 127
Singularity, 124
Slang, 55
Sleep, 128
Smiles, Samuel, 3
Smollet, Tobias, 57
Snowsfields, Chapel, 5
Solon, 104
Sorrow, godly, 97-8
Spelling, 63
Spinoza, 84
Spiritual life, 96ff., 116ff.
Spiritual Manifestation of Son of God, xv, 92, 119
Spirituality, Fletcher's, ix, 11, 95, 131
St Albans, 4
Stephen, Sir Leslie, 11
Stoicism, 11
Swift, Jonathan, 57
Switzerland, 3, 5, 9, 35

Taylor, Jeremy, 61

Taylor, Samuel, xvi
Temptations, 114
Terminology, obsolete, 46-7
  nonce, 48-50, 57, 59
  rare, 43, 46-8
  revival, 54-6, 106, 107-8, 116
Theological College (Trevecca), 10
Tithe, 13
Toplady, Augustus, xv, xvi, 38, 49, 72
Tradition, 79
Trials, Life's, 114-15
Trinity, 80-1
Truth, 70, 102, 103, 131
Truth, Essay on, xii, xv, 131
Tyerman, Luke, vii, viii, xi, 34, 93

Understanding, the, in piety, 102-4
Union with God, 97-8

Vindication of Wesley's Calm Address, xv, 92
Virtues, 112
Visiting, 25, 27
Vocabulary, Fletcher's, 40, 42ff., 72
Vocation, Religious, 121-2, 125
Voltaire, 84

Watchfulness in piety, 128
Wenlock, Abbey and Prior of, 13, 15
Wesley, Charles, xii, xiii, 110, 113
Wesley, John, vii, viii, ix, xv, 4, 8, 9, 10, 22, 31, 38, 42, 54, 68, 71, 92
Wesley Historical Society Proceedings, xiii, xv, xvi
Wesley, Susanna, 18
Whimsey gin (pithead), 2
Whitefield, George, 10, 42, 66
Wilkinson, 'Iron-mad', 2
Will, the, in piety, 104-7
Works, 38, 85, 87, 121
Wrekin, the, 2, 18

Young's *Night Thoughts*, 36, 39

www.ingramcontent.com/pod-product-compliance
Lightning Source LLC
Chambersburg PA
CBHW061957220426
43662CB00011B/1727